INTERFACE

by
Colm Heatley

Contributing Editor
Richard Bingham

Conclusion Chapter
written by
Richard Bingham

Project Editors
Ciarán Ó Pronntaigh
Bob Smith

Lagan Books Publishing

Belfast

Interface

Published 2004 by Lagan Books, Belfast
Copyright © 2004 Lagan Books
Photos © Anderstown News, Thomas McMullan, Pacemaker Press
A CIP catalogue for this book is available from the British Library
ISBN 1-904684-10-6
Printed and bound in the EU

About the Author

Colm Heatley is a freelance journalist who has written for *The North Belfast News* and other organisations. A native of Belfast, Colm has an intimate knowledge of several Interface areas and his experience as a reporter of such events for *The North Belfast News* gives him a unique understanding of the events covered in this book. Colm is currently in South-East Asia, researching his next writing project.

Editorial Team

Contributing Editor and author of this book's last chapter, Richard Bingham, has been a keen observer of current affairs for many years. Richard is also from Belfast and has many contacts with grassroots community workers and politicians.

Ciarán Ó Pronntaigh is editor of the Irish language daily newspaper *La* and has vast reporting experience on Irish affairs.

Bob Smith has been in the publishing industry for 18 years and has advised Lagan Books on many of its published titles.

Contents

This book is dedicated to all those who face the day-to-day challenges of living in Interface areas, regardless of religious persuasion or political beliefs.

Introduction

What you read in this book will be, to many people, a source of surprise and horror. Presented here are the voices of people (and those they democratically elect to represent them) who live in circumstances that are extremely challenging by any standards. Many of the people who casually pass comment on Interface areas have never had to confront these challenges at all, far less every day, and so one could argue that they are not qualified to judge the actions and attitudes of those who do.

The phenomenon of a divided society and its attendant interface areas is not a new one, nor is it one that is to be found only in Northern Ireland. Whatever their reason for being, there are many examples of communities becoming isolated and shunning contact with a larger community. This can be self-imposed as in the case of Serbs in present-day Kosovo or Slovaks avoiding contact with the Roma people in their own country. In other cases it can be imposed from outside, as in the case of Palestine where a process of 'cantonisation' is being imposed by the Israeli government, and becomes part of the dynamic of enforced change.

The salient point is that both communities see themselves as being totally different and separate from the other, in terms of nationality, religion, race, and even class. Europe is no more immune from this type of hatred than any other part of the world. And, inevitably, when the demarcation lines between two communities change, friction is caused.

A recurring theme throughout this book, particularly in Belfast, has been the vacation of inner city areas by the Protestant population attracted by suburban life outside traditional working-class areas. This has been accompanied by an increase in the Catholic population in these areas. This book's definition of "Interface" is: where a split community, or two communities come across each other, whether that be in a geographical sense where two areas meet one another, or where the two communities come into contact when there is a march.

What gives this phenomenon added impetus is the cost to human lives, the constant feeling of threat that many of those interviewed here refer to. There are many harrowing accounts of children being put on tranquillisers, terrible attacks on innocent victims, families living in terror because of never-ending attacks, nightly rioting and communities being cut off from the rest of society. As so often happens, it is the most vulnerable who come off worst in these abnormal circumstances.

In such circumstances it is not surprising that there will be a great gulf between feelings and facts. Because either one, or both communities, feel they are under threat the situation is often seen starkly as one of 'them' and 'us'. Indeed, a lot of those interviewed here admit as much, a feeling that can be seen as understandable.

Allied to this is a campaign of vilification which reduces 'the other side' to little more than vermin. Again, this can be understood, as the only physical contact that people have with the other side is a wholly negative one. It is in this context that security walls, or as they are euphemistically called, 'peace walls', have been erected, although the real reasons for their erection are explored by a number of people here.

Sometimes the walls have appeared as a stopgap measure but invariably they have become the only 'solution' to what has seemed an intractable problem.

That said, in a strange way these areas also offer something which is very lacking with other groups. That is a profound sense of community, allied, quite often with a strong sense of place and identity. It is no accident that flags proliferate at these interface areas.

These separate communities have frequently developed in parallel, each equipped with its own set of amenities and services. However, things have not always worked out to plan and as the boundaries shift many communities find themselves with their amenities on the other side of their 'no man's land'.

One of the major issues which this book deals with is

the issue of marching. These marches almost totally involve the Loyal Orders; The Orange Order, The Apprentice Boys and the Black Preceptory and their right, as they see it, to march in areas that have a nationalist majority. Nationalists in these areas demand the right to be consulted over such marches while the Loyal Orders say that it is a right that is non-negotiable and that even when talks do in fact take place they go nowhere.

Again perception plays a great part in this question. Agreements have been tantalisingly close in many cases, particularly on the Garvaghy Road but, according to one source in this book, political considerations have taken precedence and progress was stymied. The issue of trust is one that acts as a gauge as to how successful attempts to provide a settlement are. Mostly however trust is totally lacking.

The outlook for the marching issue in recent times has begun to look a lot better. Summer 2003 has been one of the most peaceful with reports of behind the scene negotiations in a number of areas. Indeed the DUP, a party which prides itself on its hard-line Unionist stance has lead the way in Derry City in trying to ensure a peaceful settlement of the marching issue.

Many other questions are raised and tackled in this book; the role of the Police Service of Northern Ireland (PSNI) the paramilitaries, social conditions and even the effect rain has on what has become known as 'recreational rioting'.

This book does ask the political leaders in the areas

how they feel the situation came to be the way it is and also to seek what answers they have to these problems.

One thing which must be kept in mind at all times is that these interface areas represent only a very small part of the population but whenever certain conditions are met most people react in similar ways. The interface syndrome is not a genetic disease but rather a way people have of dealing with a situation which has been thrust upon them. People living only a mile or two away often know very little about what life is like further up the road.

The author and the publishers would like to thank all those who made themselves available for interview in this book and who chose to speak candidly about what was happening in their areas. Whatever their views, they should be commended for their frankness. It would have been easy for all of them to have given politically correct answers and to have evaded the issue. The reader is the best judge as to whether this occurs throughout but the contributors spoke with a level of honesty which is invaluable if we are ever to gain some understanding as to why two communities can become engulfed by events such as Holy Cross and Drumcree. This book does not claim to contain all the answers, or to be a comprehensive academic study of communities in conflict, but we do hope that we have managed to bring together a wide range of opinion, covering the main issues involved in Interface areas.

Ciarán Ó Pronntaigh
Editor

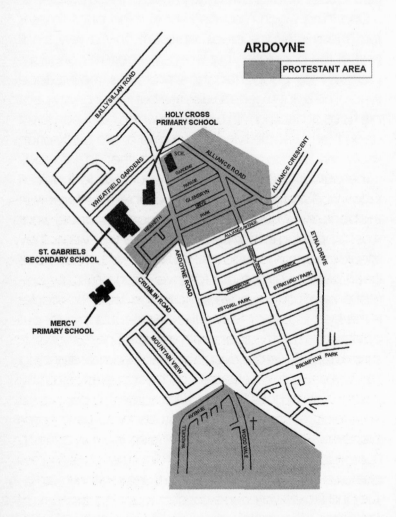

ARDOYNE

PROTESTANT AREA

BALLYSILLAN ROAD

HOLY CROSS
PRIMARY SCHOOL

WHEATFIELD GARDENS

ALLIANCE ROAD

ALLIANCE CRESCENT

SCH.

GARDENS

PARADE

GLENBRYN

DRIVE

PARK

HESKETH

ALLIANCE AVENUE

ETNA DRIVE

ST. GABRIELS
SECONDARY SCHOOL

CRUMLIN ROAD

ARDOYNE ROAD

BERWICK ROAD

KERRERA

DEVENISH

CRANBROOK

STRATHROY PARK

MERCY
PRIMARY SCHOOL

ESTORIL PARK

MOUNTAIN VIEW

BROMPTON PARK

WOODVALE

AVENUE

WOOD VALE

12

Chapter One
Alliance Avenue and Holy Cross Dispute

Alliance Avenue, in north Belfast, is undoubtedly one of the most infamous and bloodiest streets in Northern Ireland. Throughout 30 years of the Troubles almost 20 people have been killed there by loyalists, the IRA and the British Army. A narrow street of just over 100 houses it is the dividing line between the republican Ardoyne estate and the small loyalist enclave of Glenbryn.

In a troubled society the street exemplifies the divisions that mark out Belfast from other European cities. Now exclusively Catholic it was, until the Troubles began, a mixed street. In 1971 the British Army had erected a makeshift peace line to separate Alliance Avenue from Glenbryn. By the late 1980's the peace line stood 40 foot high and was a permanent feature of life for residents on both sides, with dialogue between the Catholics and Protestants who live within touching distance of the peace line virtually non-existent. It is the dividing line, the frontier, between Protestant and Catholic Ardoyne.

Catholic Ardoyne is now almost entirely fenced in by peace lines. Apart from the partition at Alliance Avenue, a wall some 300 yards long, constructed by the Northern Ireland Office (NIO), blocks off Ardoyne from the Crumlin Road. In the early 1980's Ardoyne houses on the fringe of the Crumlin Road were knocked down, as were homes and shops on the Protestant side. None were ever rebuilt, creating a wasteland. To the untrained eye the wall looks unremarkable, almost as though it should be there, but it was created with the sole intention of separating Catholic and Protestant.

One aspect of peace lines in Belfast is the form and shape they are given. The wall on the Crumlin Road has been beautified with ornate carvings and plants to make it look somehow natural. However, people from Ardoyne resent both the wall and the buffer zone, which started to grow. In effect the area is encircled by security walls of one sort or another. And, of course, Protestants on their side of the peace line similarly resent this obstacle to normal activity.

Mutual distrust, suspicions and sectarian tensions characterize the two communities' relationship and these tensions burst onto the surface dramatically in June 2001 in the form of the Holy Cross protest. Scenes of frightened Catholic schoolgirls running a gauntlet of abuse from loyalist protesters as they walked past the Glenbryn estate to get to their school captured world headlines. In a protest marked out, even by the North's standards, for its bigotry and viciousness, few could comprehend the scenes on the TV screens.

Protestants from Glenbryn insisted the schoolgirls would not be able to walk past their estate to get to school because, they claimed, the IRA was gathering intelligence in this way. The Catholic parents were equally adamant that their girls should be allowed to get to school in the quickest way possible, comparing the protesters to the white supremacists of 1950's Alabama. While an alternative route was available, many Catholic parents refused to use it, asking why should they have to 'use the back door', which to them symbolised second-class citizenship. To many Protestants however, such reasoning was unconvincing. Fraser Agnew, Independent Unionist MLA for North Belfast points out that in many instances, Unionists have had to employ practical measures to avoid conflict.

"For years, when using our Orange hall in what is now a Catholic area, we had to use the back door to avoid confrontation with local residents. And we didn't complain, it was just what we had to do."

Despite the best efforts of mediators, politicians and churchmen, the Holy Cross protest lasted for the best part of a year before it was resolved. Protestants claim the protest began when two loyalists putting up paramilitary flags at the Ardoyne Road were attacked by Catholics. They said a car rammed the two men and both narrowly escaped injury. People from Ardoyne have always strenuously denied the claim, saying no such incident took place. They accuse Protestants of seeking an excuse for the violence that followed.

In the 12 months after the protest ended Alliance Avenue was the scene of near nightly rioting between Protestants and Catholics. The PSNI (The Police Service of Northern Ireland, the name of the reformed Royal Ulster Constabulary, the RUC) were called to deal with scores of bomb attacks on Catholic homes, and more than a dozen families applied to move out of the street because of sectarian intimidation. Sixteen Catholic families, some who had lived there since the early 1980's, applied for government grants to move out because their lives were in direct danger. Protestants on the other hand equally claimed vulnerability because of attacks on their homes.

The Holy Cross protest was, however, the latest stage in a thirty year conflict of daily grinding battles between the communities living along the Alliance Avenue and Glenbryn peace line. The Holy Cross protests heightened sectarian tensions across the North in a way not seen since the Drumcree stand-off in 1996. For more than six months loyalists blocked the road to the Holy Cross Girls' Primary School.

By a quirk of history the Catholic girls' school, which draws most of its students from Ardoyne, sits opposite the loyalists Glenbryn estate. To get to the school parents and children have to walk past the housing estate, but there was never any loyalist protests outside it even during the worst of the Troubles. But now scores of PSNI officers lined the road to allow the parents and children access to the school, as hundreds of loyalists protesters jeered and threw stones while the children walked by.

On 1 September 2001, the protest took a further violent twist when a loyalist threw a pipe bomb at PSNI officers as the children neared the school gates. The device exploded and injured two policemen and a police dog. After the incident the PUP's Billy Hutchinson said he was ashamed to be a loyalist. However, he says he continued to stand with the protesters every morning to show leadership.

Anne Bill is a community worker and mother-of-two from Glenbryn. She was centrally involved in the Holy Cross protest, standing daily with the protesters and giving TV and radio interviews to defend their cause. She has no regrets about taking part. For her the Holy Cross protest had its roots in Protestant and loyalist disillusionment with the Good Friday Agreement.

"Community relations throughout all of Northern Ireland took a step backward because Protestants felt they weren't getting a fair deal under the Good Friday Agreement. People in Glenbryn kept telling the Government about attacks on their houses and how vulnerable they felt but we weren't being listened to. That is why people protested on the Ardoyne Road, the focus wasn't so much the school itself. You can't detach the Holy Cross protest from the high-level politics that go on in Northern Ireland. People on the streets see politicians at each other's throats, so it's little won-der they give up all hope of resolving local disputes in a peaceful manner. The community in Glenbryn is in decline and it is fearful of Ardoyne. That does encour-age a siege mentality. Glenbryn had no choice but to protest and I don't think people should apologise for that. If I had been a Holy Cross parent I definitely wouldn't have taken my child up through that protest, I would have walked in the back gates."

But despite Anne Bill's assertion that the protest was aimed at the British Government it was the children and parents of Holy Cross Primary who suffered the trauma and violence of that protest. During the dis-pute people in Ardoyne became increasingly frus-trated with the lack of progress in resolving it. Every morning the parents and children would line up at the junction of the Ardoyne Road and Alliance Avenue to be escorted to the school gates by police officers in riot gear. Parents resented being forced to line up and although the police stopped the protesters from get-ting within touching distance of the children abuse was still hurled.

The PSNI and the then Secretary of State, John Reid's response to the protesters angered parents and the Holy Cross Board of Governors. A Holy Cross parent sought a judicial review of the PSNI behaviour at the protest. The parent's solicitor argued that the PSNI had afforded the children and protesters equal protec-tion when in fact the children had a greater right to get to school freely than the protesters had to protest. At the time of writing the result of the judicial review was still pending.

The gauntlet which had to be run was indeed daunting. Loyalists took to blowing foghorns and whistles as the children walked by, creating a frightening din. And parents claimed that some of the protesters held up pornographic images as the children walked by and sometimes urine was thrown. The pressure and tensions caused by the protest were exacerbated by the nightly violence.

One of the central figures in negotiating a resolution was Fr. Aidan Troy who arrived as parish priest in Ardoyne shortly before the Holy Cross dispute began. As head of the Board of Governors at the school he showed his solidarity with the parents and children by walking with them to school every day. Fr. Troy was a Catholic priest of some thirty years and head of the Passionist Order in Europe having served in war-torn countries such as Rwanda and the Congo. 'A Baptism of fire' is how he describes coming to Ardoyne.

"I really found it hard to comprehend the hatred that was shown to the school girls. It shocked me and I felt such pity for these little school girls who were being exposed to such hatred on a daily basis. I walked with them and because of that I was spat on by the protesters. They held up posters accusing me of being a paedophile and they showed the children pornographic images. The intensity of the protest was hard to comprehend; I don't think people can really understand that from watching it on television. It was a brutal period of time when every morning and every afternoon was an ordeal for the parents and the children. Everyone in the community was affected by it, but the parents and the children showed great dignity in coming through it. I remember seeing fathers and grandfathers walking up with their little girls and all sorts of abuse was being hurled at them. They must have been tempted to take the law into their own hands but they maintained a dignity and a courage that is rarely seen."

North Belfast Independent Unionist MLA, Fraser Agnew concedes that he too was "appalled by the gauntlet of hate" that developed.

"The protests at Holy Cross were self-defeating. I understood why they were taking place. I wouldn't say that all Protestant violence was reactionary but a lot of it was. What happened at Holy Cross was a reaction to the fact that Protestant residents were denied access to local facilities [in Ardoyne] such as shops, Post Offices, children's playgrounds, etc. They were denied the most basic rights by pure intimidation. People were actually attacked, including pensioners. And Protestants genuinely felt that this was an orchestrated campaign to drive them from Ardoyne and that absolutely nothing was being done about this. And this campaign was under the control of so-called community workers – and the message was 'get the Prods out of Ardoyne'.

"I could take you to the Serpentine Road and show you where children going to the Ballygolan School there had to run a similar gauntlet of hate.

"What annoyed me so much about Holy Cross was that in the end there were more Provos walking that road than children. It really was 'putting it up' to you. What sort of parent would put their child through that?"

In the first two weeks of the protest that restarted in September 2001, 15 children left the school and there were reports that the school would have to close because of falling numbers.

Meetings between the Board of Governors and the protesting Glenbryn residents, who were then known as CRUA (Concerned Residents of Upper Ardoyne) took place. In total five face-to-face meetings were held but little progress was made. Fr. Troy describes the meetings as difficult and says the structure of CRUA presented problems.

"The meetings never descended to any personal abuse but they were most certainly difficult. We also felt that the whole way in which CRUA went about making their decisions hampered the whole process. They had to report back to the entire community and tell them what was going on. That left them open to being forced out of any decisions they were going to take and so progress was very slow. We had our final meeting a few weeks before the protests ended and we wanted to discuss how we would approach security of the children and the parents. But that was the last time we had any contact with them during the protest."

Tentative steps to restore relations in the wake of the protest were made through the North Belfast Community Action Unit. Set up to foster inter-community talks it focuses on social and economic issues of interest to Ardoyne and Glenbryn. Nevertheless, community workers from both sides admit progress has been slow. Anne Bill, who is regarded as one of the more moderate voices in Glenbryn, says her counterparts in Ardoyne are hard to take at face value.

"On the occasions when we meet with them I always get the feeling that they are playing games with us. I have met people from other republican areas of the city and they always seem more genuine. I don't know if that is because we have so much conflict with Ardoyne or whether that is the way they actually are but it shows that relations are pretty bad."

Comments such as these highlight a fundamental feature of Interface areas – that people in these situations hold such a well-honed suspicion of their nearest neighbours, their nearest 'threat', that they see them as uniquely distrustful and untrustworthy. And so these people have more time for absolutely anyone else over them. This seems to be a universal trait in such circumstances, regardless of rights and wrongs.

One of the effects of the Holy Cross dispute was the demarcation of territory along the interface. The Ardoyne Road which connects Glenbryn to Catholic

Ardoyne was festooned with flags and emblems at either end. On the Catholic side tricolours were flown from lampposts, while at the loyalists end UDA flags, Union Jacks and even Israeli flags fluttered. Fraser Agnew acknowledges this territorial aspect of the North Belfast situation in general and the Holy Cross dispute in particular. He also suggests that this aspect is more pronounced as a result of one feature of The Belfast Agreement.

"There is a battle for territory in all of this, where you get paramilitaries on both sides trying to control areas for their own criminal reasons and both sides hide under the cloak of their supposed causes. One of the problems of the Good Friday Agreement was that prisoner releases put many of these people back on the streets free to intimidate their areas."

While the dispute was eventually brought to an end, the street violence, however, continued. In ending the dispute the Glenbryn residents said they would await the outcome of a report by the First and Deputy First Ministers of Northern Ireland. They wanted the report to recommend a security gate be erected at the junction of Alliance Avenue and the Ardoyne Road. The report was also to deal with traffic calming measures and greater security measures for the Glenbryn area. Holy Cross parents had always opposed a security gate saying it would cut the school off from Ardoyne and leave them vulnerable to attack. In the event the report did not recommend a

gate be built but the loyalists were prepared to accept this although the protesters referred to the ending of the protests as 'suspension'.

But the Glenbryn residents' refusal to rule out another
protest added to a sense of insecurity in Ardoyne. Parents and the Holy Cross Board of Governors wanted
loyalists to definitively rule out any further protest outside the school, something they refused to do.

A month before the protest was called off the Department of Social Development announced a housing redevelopment package for Glenbryn. This move
infuriated nationalists, particularly in north Belfast, where
almost 80% of people on the housing waiting list are
Catholics. They viewed the package as a buy-off for
Glenbryn residents. Ardoyne Sinn Féin councillor
Margaret McClenaghan says the common perception was that loyalists were being rewarded for intimidating schoolgirls.

"The money involved in the housing package and
the way it was announced meant people could only
reach one conclusion, that loyalists were being bought
off. They refused to listen to reason to call off their protest so the British government simply bought them off
with cash. Nationalist housing in north Belfast is chroni-
cally overcrowded and under-funded, yet here we are
with Glenbryn having millions pumped into it."

One Protestant community activist expressed a different perspective.

"There is no victory for our area despite all the hype.

It is actually a strategy of social political engineering between the NIO and the Housing Executive, to solve the issue of interface tension.

"Initially, two streets of Glenbryn, 186 houses, will be demolished in so called 'redevelopment'. At most, about 20% will be replaced. Once the original residents have been dispersed they will have settled elsewhere and will not be able to return, as too few houses will be available. A less viable Protestant community, reducing in numbers with further demolition, will be more vunerable to republican attacks. Inevitably, there will be a complete exodus of Protestants due to fear and intimidation, as has happened in other interface areas. And 'Hey Presto!' Problem solved. Go for the soft option. Move the Protestants! In essence, we have covert collusion between Sinn Féin and Number 10, in order to solve an embarrassing issue.

"It is very rich for Fr. Troy and others to insist that parents and children have a right to walk to school along a disputed route with as much security protection as necessary, even when well-known IRA men were walking with them, blatantly exploiting the situation. Can you imagine the police escorting Michael Stone through the Short Strand!

"When Protestant kids and parents were being attacked going to Everton School on the Crumlin Road, Police and Army support was evident for a while. But as soon as IRA snipers began murdering RUC and army, a decision was taken to close the school. And it is now a Health Centre. The rights of those kids were taken away. Where is the consistency in dealing with the two communities?"

Dr Pete Shirlow of the University of Ulster who has researched interface areas in Belfast says that housing disputes are a key component of such disputes.

"It can even boil down to things like how big a garden is. For instance in Protestant areas there are more houses than people to fill them so when the Housing Executive redevelops them they tend to build them with bigger gardens and more space around them because the volume of housing isn't so important. But when nationalists look at this they see Protestants getting luxury houses while they are living in overcrowded and cramped conditions."

For months after the Holy Cross protest ended police and British Army Land Rovers and Saracens sat outside the school and at the junction of Alliance Avenue, but eventually parents were able to walk their children to school without a police and army escort. Fr. Aidan Troy describes the weeks and months after the protest as tense.

"Understandably parents still felt that they were very vulnerable to attack in the weeks afterward. No-one knew for sure what was going to happen but at least the immediate pressure of the protest was off. For the first time the parents weren't walking up in double file and altogether at set times. They could walk up freely and the children didn't have to huddle beside their parents. I can still remember the night the protest was called off. It wasn't until around midnight that the residents said the protest wouldn't be going ahead the next day. There was great sense of relief and joy and of sadness. People were crying, it was the build-up of pressure over months when they were just trying to keep their heads above water. During the protest some of the schoolgirls had been put on heavy tranquillizers such as Diazepam. Kids as young as eight and nine were actually on tranquillisers because of the trauma they were experiencing in their own homes and going to school in the morning."

Parents told how their children had been wetting the bed and had started to throw tantrums and become withdrawn. When teachers in the Holy Cross school asked P6 girls to draw a picture many had drawn mothers and fathers crying, surrounded by people with angry faces.

Brendan Bradley heads the nearby Survivors of Trauma group which deals with victims of violence throughout the Troubles. He says that the trauma experienced by the children is almost without parallel in the history of the Troubles.

"What is amazing about this is the fact that the girls, some were only four years old, were subjected to abuse and protest every day and every afternoon they went to school. It wasn't as though this abuse lasted for a couple of days or was a one-off, it went on for months. Many needed counselling, some long-term counselling, in the wake of it all. Parents told how their daughters had changed from being fun-loving to being very withdrawn."

The trauma posed by the protest was made worse because some of the children lived in Alliance Avenue, which was itself the scene of nightly riots. Houses along the peace line with Glenbryn were attacked with pipe bombs and petrol bombs. Roisin Keenan lived on Alliance Avenue during the Holy Cross protest. Some time afterwards she moved out of the area after a third bomb attack on her house. Her only daughter Fionnuala was just three-years-old and in the Holy Cross playgroup when the protest began in June. Every day until the end of November mother and daughter walked up the Ardoyne Road through the protests. But Roisin says the continual attacks on her house at night-time made her time in Alliance Avenue a living hell.

"At the time I thought Fionnuala would be too young to be affected by the protest but I was very wrong. Looking back I don't know how we did it, how we actually managed to walk through that wall of noise and protest and hatred every morning of life. I think it is only afterwards when you look at a situation that you realise the stress you were under. We took her to the playgroup and it was funny because you nearly expected to see the same faces shouting at you every morning. But I don't think we could have coped if it had have went on for much longer."

Roisin's home was attacked with stones and petrol bombs on countless occasions, twice with pipe bombs which exploded in her backyard and once with a hoax device. Eventually she was only able to sell her house through the Special Purchase of Evacuated Dwellings Scheme, a government scheme which buys houses from people who were victims of intimidation and designed to ensure they receive the full market value for their property. When the first attacks on Alliance Avenue started in April the upper part of the street where Roisin lived was not protected by a peace line. The peace line at the top of Alliance wasn't built until five months later. Until then her tormentors could climb through her hedge.

Another feature of interface conflict is the confusing maze of claim and counterclaim, not just relating to incidents that have taken place, but also as to whether certain incidents took place at all. For instance, Glenbryn residents complain about a BBC report based on a Sinn Féin claim that 200 loyalists had attacked Catholic homes, which the residents insist never happened. The police confirmed the resident's denial. Such are the levels of suspicion across Northern Ireland however that many Catholics would, rightly or wrongly, expect the police to 'back up' loyalist claims.

It is a common assertion in Protestant areas that the media is frequently 'hoodwinked' by republican propaganda. Some loyalists would go further and suggest that certain elements of the so-called 'independent' media are actually nationalist sympathisers not being hoodwinked at all but are wilfully putting their own slant on events. Whatever the truth, most loyalist communities resent their portrayal in the reporting of interface areas, believing that their side almost always comes off worse.

News organisations would deny such suggestions vigorously and would claim to be alive to the manipulations of competing propaganda. But with the facts often difficult to state with certainty, a reporter's own judgement often plays a bigger part in the report than he/she intended. And while that judgement might be utterly impartial, both republican and loyalist communities can feel alienated by the judgements of people who do not face the same daily challenges as they do.

Three decades of violence have created a climate of fear, where suspicion, mistrust and resentment of each community grew. To many the 40-foot-high peace line was the British Government's crude response to those problems. The British Government argues the peace lines are a security measure designed to protect lives and stop riots. Gerard McGuigan is a community worker in Ardoyne. He was one of the first Sinn Féin councillors elected to Belfast City Council and has lived in Ardoyne all his life. He says that when the peace lines first went up in 1971 few people took much notice of them.

"At that stage it was non-stop riots with the Brits; people weren't thinking of the future and nobody thought the conflict would last until the 1990's. The Brits were taking over empty houses in Alliance Avenue and using them as observation posts so a fence here and there seemed insignificant. The Alliance Avenue peace line just grew like a tree. Once it started going up people started testing it for weak spots and that led to it being extended further. A lot of the time the peace line was actually no more than a rickety fence, there were holes all over it and it was more symbolic than practical. To understand the peace lines you have to understand the early days of the Troubles and the population shifts that were taking place. Catholics were being burned out of their houses and Protestants were consolidating their own strongholds. But what the peace lines did was to consolidate divisions without actually offering people much security. In 2003 Catholics in Alliance Avenue are still being attacked by loyalists on a regular basis. No Catholic in Alliance Avenue has ever felt safe from loyalist attack and you just have to look at the number killed there to see why."

Gerard McGuigan feels that the peace lines make it more difficult for the Catholic community in Ardoyne to grow naturally.

"I'm not saying the peace lines haven't offered the residents a degree of security, even if in many ways that was mainly psychological. But they have also added to a feeling that the two communities don't need to talk to each other. You have to remember that the DUP still doesn't talk to Sinn Féin and that mentality filters down to their own people on the interfaces. People should also remember that the peace lines never stopped attacks. In fact UDA gunmen in Glenbryn would use the wall as cover to fire into Ardoyne on the Twelfth of July. They could hide behind the fence and launch attacks and if nationalists came out the British Army and RUC would swamp the area and begin raiding Protestant houses.

"And during the late 80's the loyalists would drive down Alliance Avenue, pick a house and try and kill anyone inside. Within twenty seconds they were back in their own area."

One such attack claimed the life of 63-year-old father of 13, David Braniff. A Protestant convert to Catholicism he was shot dead by the UVF as he knelt saying the Rosary in his Alliance Avenue home in March 1989. Even after the ceasefires of 1994 people continued to be murdered in Alliance Avenue. On 31 October 1998 Brian Service, a 35-year-old Catholic, was shot dead by loyalist gunmen as he walked along Alliance Avenue. He was the last victim of violence that year. Such attacks reinforced the fear factor for Catholics living in Alliance Avenue.

In common with most interface areas both Ardoyne and Glenbryn suffer from high levels of socio-economic deprivation.

A report carried out by the University of Ulster in 1992 showed that 69% of people living in interface areas earned less than £5,000 annually, compared to a Northern Ireland average of 45%. Thirty-one percent of the community was unemployed, compared with a Northern Ireland average of 14% and 41% received income support, compared with an average of 21%.

An undeniable aspect of the violence around interface areas centres on perceived territorial expansion. Perhaps surprisingly, given the record of attacks against Catholics in Alliance Avenue, it is the loyalist side that is most keen to see the peace line extended. One of the key demands made by the Holy Cross protestors was the erection of a security gate at the junction of Alliance Avenue and the Ardoyne Road, the invisible border between Catholic and Protestant Ardoyne. In effect the gate would have meant Glenbryn would be almost entirely cut-off from the rest of Ardoyne.

Protestants are also most keen to have the height of the peace line raised. According to North Belfast MLA, Billy Hutchinson, a leading member of the UVF-aligned Progressive Unionist Party, this is because Protestants fear Catholics are intent on driving them out of the area. It is a view shared among Protestants across the North, leading them to adopt a siege mentality and view any outward sign of compromise as a devilish ruse dreamt up by republicans. Demographic changes in north Belfast mean that Protestants there feel the pinch of a dwindling population more than most. Between 1981 and 1997 the Protestant electorate in north Belfast has shrunk by almost 20,000. Since the ceasefires of 1994 Glenbryn's population has plummeted from more than 3,000 people to just over 900, according to community workers in the area. That decline is symptomatic of working-class Protestant areas. For example, in 1969 72,000 people lived in the Greater Shankill area, by 1996 there were only 20,000 left.

Community workers in the Shankill area explain that this decline is due to massive demolition of many streets by The Northern Ireland Housing Executive, with only a fraction being replaced, despite promises to the contrary.

The rise in Sinn Féin's vote in North Belfast has also had a disconcerting effect on Unionists. In the 1992 Westminster elections Sinn Féin polled 4,693 votes in North Belfast or 13.1% of the vote. In the 2001 Westminster elections Sinn Féin polled 10,331 votes or 25.2% of the vote. The population shift and the emergence of a nationalist consensus are critical to understanding why territorial disputes are central to the conflicts that surround peace lines.

The end of industries which traditionally employed Protestants, such as the Harland and Wolff shipyard, and the availability of cheaper and better housing on the outskirts of Belfast have tempted many Protestants to move from areas such as the Shankill and Glenbryn. However, Unionist and loyalist politicians prefer to see demographic changes as part of a republican conspiracy to drive them from their areas. Billy Hutchinson says loyalists in Glenbryn feel under siege.

"If you look at Glenbryn it is really a very small community surrounded by a much larger republican one. People there are hemmed in and they see Ardoyne expanding constantly. Continual talk of the rising nationalist population makes people feel that even more. To Protestants in Glenbryn it feels that if they give away any more ground they will be wiped out as a community. People there are always on the defensive and feel their plight is ignored. The protest was a disaster in terms of putting their cause forward but it was a genuine expression of their anger and frustration and fear over what is happening in that part of North Belfast."

However, Billy Hutchinson rejects the view that Protestant areas are in demographic decline because of republican aggression.

"I think it has more to do with economics and the loss of centres of employment than anything else. What has happened in Glenbryn is typical of Protestant areas all over Belfast. Since the late 1960's Protestants have been moving to the outskirts of Belfast so it isn't surprising that today there is a lot of dereliction in inner-city working-class areas. It is definitely true though that Unionism in general has felt less confident for the last 35 years than it ever has done. People are apprehensive about the future, they don't know what it is going to bring and often that fear can manifest itself in violence. Before the cease-fires that anger expressed itself in shootings and bombings, and even if people didn't go out and join organisations like the UVF or the UDA they felt that their interests were being looked after by them. Since 1994 people haven't had that and I believe that is part of the reason for the rise in sectarianism at the interfaces. No-one is going out and doing the shoot-ings or the bombings so people from interface areas are more likely to vent their anger on each other. The sectarianism that exists in the upper-class parlours of Cultra and places like it is no less vile than the bigotry that exists in working-class areas. With the middle-classes it might find expression in the form of discrimi-nation in jobs but working-class people don't have those resources so the only expression of it is to riot and to inflict pain and violence on each other."

Sinn Féin's Gerry Kelly, a North Belfast MLA (with para-military convictions as has Hutchinson) says the vio-lence surrounding Glenbryn and the Holy Cross block-ade are a microcosm of the whole conflict in the North. As the senior Sinn Féin member for North Belfast he was involved in behind-the-scenes negotiations with the parents of the Holy Cross children and with com-munity leaders from Ardoyne.

"Over the past four or five years the focus of conflict

has switched to interface areas in Belfast. This has meant attacks on homes on a nightly basis and the re-emergence of the UDA on the streets, directing these riots and attacks. The UDA used the Holy Cross blockade and other interface areas as a way to destabilise the peace process, to try and derail it. Their tactics were very simple – to cause enough instability on the streets to make sure political progress couldn't happen. Trying to resolve it took up a lot of time for a lot of people. I was working at Stormont during the day, when I could, and going to Ardoyne at night time to try and stop the trouble, that cycle went on for more than a year and it was clear what the intent behind it was."

Fraser Agnew, the Independent Unionist MLA for North Belfast agrees with the statement that "there has been a orchestrated pipe-bombing campaign by loyalists against Catholics, designed to intimidate them out of their homes in North Belfast". However, he adds that a similar situation existed in reverse in Whitewell and Short Strand, where Protestant residents were under attack. He accepted that Catholics there might see it differently but he insisted that there was validity in the Protestant perception that they too were 'under siege' in certain areas.

Agnew accepts that his analysis might not seem fair to nationalists but he felt that as an elected representative, elected by Protestants, that his first responsibility was to fulfil the leadership function of bringing like-minded people with him. He appreciates that this logic also applies to republicans and this is why republicans can seem unreasonable to unionists. And this may be why republicans do not go as far as Unionists would like on issues such as condemning republican rioters and decommissioning. He further points out that in North Belfast, the INLA and CIRA are waiting in the wings, hoping that the 'Provos' would take one step too far and leave 'their people' behind and so he appreciates the constraints on them.

Sometimes the violence had a destabilising effect on the political manoeuvrings in Stormont. On one occasion republican gunmen shot and wounded a Protestant youth from Glenbryn during the height of a riot. He was badly injured in the leg. Unionist politicians demanded the Secretary of State revoke the IRA's ceasefire status and ban Sinn Féin from office. However the source of the gunfire could not be definitely proved and the calls came to nothing.

For Gerry Kelly one of the key factors contributing to the violence is the DUP's refusal to talk to republicans.

"The DUP have refused to negotiate with Sinn Féin for the past 30 years. Even now, almost ten years into a peace process, they are still doing the same thing and that is very dangerous. They are sending out the message to loyalists that it is okay not to talk; in fact it is better not to talk. Now if people close down dialogue as an option in a conflict situation then one of the other options that become viable is to engage

in violence. They are effectively working against rec-
onciliation and the UDA is using that idea to encour-
age attacks and violence."

Despite the divisions both sides agree that Ardoyne
and Glenbryn would benefit in the long-term if the
peace lines were taken down. However, no-one can
agree on how that will happen or the conditions that
will lead to it.

One measure adopted to improve mutual security at the Interface Area was to install surveillance
cameras. But though that was welcomed by
Glenbryn Residents, Sinn Féin spokesmen objected
as they saw it as an 'intrusion' on their community's
privacy. Several were latter cut down by gangs wield-
ing angle grinders.

Alban Maginness of the moderately nationalist SDLP
and the first Catholic Lord Mayor of Belfast when he
took the post in 1998, says the peace lines are a
sign of failure. And he says that if the governments
can't get it right at the Ardoyne interface they can't
get it right anywhere. As north Belfast's most senior
SDLP member he argues the spread of the peace
lines went almost unnoticed during the height of the
Troubles, creating no-go areas for Catholics and
Protestants.

"Before the Troubles a lot of what are now termed
the interface areas of Belfast would have been mixed.
Areas such as Newington and Ardoyne would have
been home to Catholics and Protestants. Although

people thought of areas in terms of Protestant and Catholic there would have been much less segregation. Today in north Belfast almost every area is either predominantly Protestant or Catholic. We really need to find a way out of that situation but there are no easy answers. Violence destroys communities and in my opinion a lot of the violence that happened in the past two years could have been avoided. If the police and army had been much more pro-active in trying to stop loyalists, from where the great majority of the violence was emanating, then it would all have been over much quicker. What happened at Holy Cross was wholly unacceptable but what is happening all over Belfast is that sectarianism is on the rise."

The wall which separates Ardoyne from the Crumlin Road is supplemented by a permanent security gate at the bottom of Flax Avenue. In the 1980's Orange Bands would stop at the Protestant side of the gate to bang their drums and play loud renditions of the Sash. Riots frequently broke out.

Michael Liggett is a community worker in Ardoyne. He says the wall has inhibited the development of Ardoyne as a community.

"We are hemmed in on all sides, we can't stretch out and grow like other communities. The problem isn't a lack of space; it is the peace wall, if that is what you want to call it, keeping us ringed in. Most of the Crumlin road lies derelict and part of Ardoyne itself has been chopped off to create a buffer zone. Overnight streets that housed hundreds of people were literally cut from the map because of British security considerations. Where does that leave this community? We have a chronic housing need in this part of north Belfast but our community is totally enclosed by walls, it means that new houses can't be built and when they are it is a question of taking away what little free land there is for more housing. That means kids have absolutely nowhere to go and play. We are supposed to be in a peace process at this point and it is time for the walls to come down. Or is the British Government telling us that they think loyalists are still going to come in and try to assassinate us?"

Although people in Ardoyne object to the security wall which runs along the Crumlin Road it has meant loyalist gunmen have had greater difficulty in targeting nationalists from the area. Likewise Protestants living in the streets behind the wall on their side of the road give reluctant support for such protection as the wall provides against attacks from Catholics. From the early 1970's, both republican and loyalists gunmen emerged from their own side of where the peace line now is and inflicted terror on the other side's community.

The Crumlin Road is regarded as one of the most dangerous roads in north Belfast. It gained its grizzly reputation in the 1970's when loyalists from the nearby Shankill would cruise along in cars looking for unsuspecting Catholic victims. In the late 1970's it became a pick up zone for the infamous Shankill Butchers Gang. Victims were bundled into cars in the dead of night before being taken away for torture sessions at the hands of the notorious UVF gang.

Although today most of the paramilitary violence that blighted this part of North Belfast has disappeared, both communities still live in fear. An uneasy peace exists, particularly during evening hours. Protestants behind their side of the wall still complain of regular assaults with missiles thrown over the wall, or direct attacks by nationalists using Protestant pedestrian access in the wall and retreating back to their own territory.

One direct result of these attacks has caused problems for a local housing association, which has difficulty allocating houses adjacent to the peace line wall, despite a pressing housing need in that Protestant area.

Residents say that the reluctance of the police to pursue the intruders into the Ardoyne has only compounded Protestant insecurity.

• • • • • • • •

If there were obvious solutions to these interface area's problems, we'd know them by now. What is apparent however from the interviews for this book is the high level of unreported grassroots activity focused on at least reducing tensions, even if a durable, mutually acceptable solution to the whole "peace line" question is as elusive as ever. This determination on the part of the communities and their elected representatives succeeded, according to many accounts, in ensuring the summer of 2003 was a little less violent then the immediately preceding years at least. Meanwhile, the fundamental issues – demographic, political, religious and national – continue to test these communities to the limits of endurance.

Chapter 2
The Whitewell and White City

Of all the peace lines in Belfast, the one separating the Protestant White City estate from the Whitewell area of north Belfast is the most surprising. Until the first Drumcree standoff in 1995 the two areas coexisted relatively peacefully with only the occasional outbreak of sectarian violence. Since then the Whitewell and White City have been the scene of frequent riots.

It is also the area where the gunmen of the UDA have been most active. The group killed two Catholics, and a Protestant mistaken for a Catholic, within a one-mile radius of White City in 2001. When the Drumcree crisis was at its height in 1996 Protestants from all over Belfast took to the streets to man barricades and confront the RUC and British Army. It was the first time since the 1994 ceasefires that political tensions had boiled over onto the streets.

For some Protestants it was a chance to show their hostility to the peace process and their fear that their rights were being steadily eroded under the new dispensation. Since October of the previous year the UVF and UFF had called off their murder campaigns against the what they saw as the republican community in the North. Of course, nationalists would point out that many victims of loyalist violence were simply Catholics, full stop. In the three years prior to the ceasefire loyalists actually outstripped the IRA in terms of murders committed. Encouraged by the ceasefires some Catholics moved to mixed districts on the edges of loyalist areas of Belfast which had been abandoned in the early days of the Troubles. The Whitewell was one such estate.

Housing shortages have always been a major issue within the Catholic community, particularly in Belfast. Between 1994 and 1995 Catholics started to trickle back into the Whitewell area, assuming they would be safe from the worst forms of sectarian violence. To some residents in the adjoining White City estate it was an unwelcome development. To make matters worse the summer of 1996 was to be one of the most violent of any during the Troubles. All over the North riots broke out, loyalists blocked roads and attacked the RUC and British Army. Unionist and loyalist political leaders demanded that their Orange brethren should be allowed to march through the nationalist Garvaghy Road in Portadown. The Orangemen had been banned from marching through the area after Catholic residents objected. But encouraged by news of loyalist roadblocks at Larne ferry access and many main roads, Protestants from White City drove a burning lorry to the entrance of their estate and within hours a confrontation had begun.

The Whitewell was traditionally a mixed community, both in terms of religion and class. During its heyday in the 1960's the area was a middle-class redoubt, nestling in the foothills above Belfast Lough. Detached bungalows and neat semidetached houses lined its sloping streets and even during the worst of the Troubles it was still a much sought after area. Catholics living there had been relatively untouched by the street trouble, which from time to time flared up in other parts of the city. Most of the UDA and UVF's murder bids were directed at the equally nearby but more working-class Catholic areas of Bawnmore and the Longlands. However, after July 1996, the mainly middle-class Catholic Whitewell and the loyalist White City estate, were embroiled in a bitter sectarian dispute that culminated in a mass exodus of people from the area in the summer of 2002. Protestants have continued to move out, claiming the area is becoming distinctly green in character while Catholics were under increased attack.

In 1999, as Europe geared up to celebrate the new millennium, a Berlin-wall style peace line was built along the boundary between the Whitewell and White City. The fence divided the two areas for 200 metres and was almost 30 feet high at its peak. It was the first peace line to be built in Belfast since 1994. At the time Adam

Ingram, then Northern Ireland Security Minister said he was reluctant to make the move.

"I have based my decision solely on the pressing need to maintain the safety of both communities living in this area. I very much regret the need to take such a decision to physically separate these two communities, particularly at a time when we are so close to an agreement on Northern Ireland's future. I believe however, there is no other option available in the circumstances. Since 1 January 1997 the police have recorded nearly 300 separate incidents in the area, the vast majority of which have been caused by the scourge of sectarianism. Despite strenuous efforts, no alternative solution to this fencing could be identified. I am aware that not everyone will agree with my decision. I believe that the measures proposed represent the best way of preserving peace and maintaining order in this area of north Belfast."

Residents from both estates requested it. However it failed to reduce the number of sectarian attacks from both sides of the divide. The nonstop riots created such a fever pitch of tension in the area that in June 2001 before the mass exodus a year later, Abigail McKeown, a Catholic mother of four deliberately ran over a 16 year-old Protestant youth named Thomas McDonald. He had been trying to smash her windscreen with a brick because he knew she was a Catholic. In February 2003 McKeown was convicted of manslaughter and sentenced to four years in jail.

There was such a surge in applications for the government sponsored SPED scheme that the government subtly changed the rules — during 2002 the police told families they were only eligible if they were threatened by name. This meant that families who had blast bombs and petrol bombs thrown over their back yard couldn't move house.

SDLP MLA Alban Maginness, who lives close to the area says the summer of 1996 was the most traumatic event of his political career.

"The sectarian violence of that year blew into a fireball – it couldn't have been controlled and it was simply ugly and frightening. The rioting got out of control and residents in the Whitewell didn't know how to cope with it. A lot of them were elderly or would have moved there to get away from that sort of trouble in the first place. After that first year everyone hoped it would all blow over and people like myself tried to work behind the scenes to get some sort of dialogue going with the Unionist community. But the next year it was just as bad and people in the area felt there was no way out of it all."

Despite the violence Alban Maginness opposed the decision to build the peace line and raised his concerns with Adam Ingram in 1999.

"I said to him it was consolidating the demarcation line in the area and that it would deepen the problem. The way to resolve the tension was through community dialogue, not building ever more barricades.

At the same time I was very much aware of community tensions in the area and at the end of it all the concerns of the residents had to take first place. In my opinion the police could have done more to stop the trouble and stop the attacks in the White City. The peace line hasn't stopped the attacks. Some of the most extreme elements of loyalism in the area used the situation around Drumcree to force Catholics out of their houses in the Whitewell. It was naked bigotry."

However within the Unionist community living in White City the fear was a familiar one - encroachment and absorption into a larger and better organised Catholic community intent on taking their houses. Three Protestant churches once stood on the Whitewell road, with another in White City itself. By the late 1990's only two were in use and the road had become predominantly Catholic, with tricolours flying from lamp posts. In 2002, Whitehouse Presbyterian Church on nearby Shore Road was completely destroyed in an arson attack. DUP councillor Nelson McCausland represented the White City area from 1989 until 2001, and was "never away from the place when it was at its worst." He is convinced that Sinn Féin has an agenda to drive all Protestants from north Belfast, and particularly from areas like the White City.

"The White City is a small vulnerable community hemmed in by nationalists. Sinn Féin quite clearly wanted to move Catholics into vacated houses on the Protestant side and create another Catholic area.

That is why they opposed putting up the peace lines while at the same time republicans were attacking Protestant homes."

He denies the trouble began when the Drumcree protests first occurred and instead points to a dwindling Protestant community in the area.

He also argues that far more resources are being poured into Catholic communities than is necessary.

"It is about the dynamics of people living together and communities coexisting. Unionists see Catholics getting all the best resources poured into their communities. For instance I estimate that for every one Protestant community worker in Belfast there are ten Catholic community workers. But Protestant communities are more fragmented than Catholic communities by nature. We don't have one church and Protestants are more independent minded so more likely to leave their areas. I have all the sympathy in the world with the people from White City, they are living on the interface and they are subjected to awful abuse. People want to defend their community, that is why the Government must help regenerate areas like the White City. Catholics and Protestants think differently," he concludes.

Some official statistics suggest that a higher level of funding and other resources are allocated to Catholic areas. This can be partly attributed to a traditionally less dynamic and less co-ordinated community activity among Protestants.

It must also be said that nationalists and indeed the Community Relations Council for Northern Ireland would hotly dispute his claim about Catholic community workers.

The trouble also presented a chance for republican splinter groups such as the Continuity IRA (CIRA) and INLA to gain support among disenchanted Catholic youths. Both groups are fundamentally opposed to the IRA ceasefire and the Good Friday Agreement. Their support is minuscule throughout Northern Ireland and it is only in areas such as the White City where they have any chance of claiming to be 'protectors of their community'.

In July 2002 CIRA gunmen made a point of 'patrolling' the Whitewell with guns on show. And the INLA followed suit, telling people they would 'protect' them at all costs. Mainstream republicans in Sinn Féin and the IRA regard such public gestures as mere bravado, an attempt to woo young nationalists. In the 1970's such republican divisions were often solved by bloody feuds. Sinn Féin's Gerry Kelly said calming people became more difficult as time went on.

"People were obviously very angry that their homes were being attacked and that they could hardly go a night without having something thrown at their houses. Tempers run high and a lot of people were enraged not only at the loyalists but the response of the PSNI to the trouble. A major part of my work there was trying to calm people. It was only through being there and through the work of community workers that we were able to do that. That became almost impossible when the PSNI and the RUC before them were firing plastic bullets at people."

According to Whitewell community worker Paul McKernon the violence that engulfed the area after the signing of the Good Friday Agreement was just part of a campaign against Catholics in the nearby Graymount Estate. Between 1997 and 1999 the small Catholic community that had lived in this estate was virtually driven out. An estimated 20 families applied to sell their houses under the SPED scheme. Paul McKernon says Catholics in the Whitewell area looked on, fearful that they would be next.

"The whole of Graymount was basically cleansed of Catholics in a two year period. House after house was attacked, within a couple of years there was no Catholic left in the area. That cannot be ignored, it was part of an ongoing campaign to drive Catholics out."

Tensions between the two communities rumbled on until 2000, when relations between them sharply deteriorated, even by Northern Ireland's standards.

Around Easter of 2000 the UDA began a pipe bomb campaign against Catholic families living on interface areas of Belfast. Such was the ferocity of the campaign that their ceasefire status was called into question by the Secretary of State, John Reid.

Three of the most recent sectarian murders were carried out within a half-mile radius of the Whitewell/White

City peace line. The murders, all carried out by the UDA/UFF, reinforced fear amongst Catholics living in the wider area. In early January 2002 Catholic postman Danny McColgan was murdered by the UDA as he stood outside the postal sorting office in the staunchly loyalist Rathcoole estate, just a few minutes drive from the Whitewell. The son of a mixed marriage, his maternal grandfather lives in the small White City estate.

Within days of the sectarian slaying graffiti reading "Danny McColgan - Postman Splat' was daubed on the walls of the estate emphasising the gulf between the two communities and further embittered young people living there. Danny McColgan's mother Marie doubts her son's killers will ever be brought to justice. She says living less than a mile from where her son's killers are based helps keep the pain alive.

"Danny just lived for his little daughter, his girlfriend and his music, that was all he ever cared about. He was the most inoffensive person you could have met and the ones who took his life away didn't care about any of that, they just cared that he was a Catholic. It has left our family heartbroken and we have no hope that those who did it will ever be brought before the courts. But that is what sectarian hatred does to people, it makes them want to kill and to take away a life."

When six months later the Unionist controlled Newtownabbey council refused to name a local park in his memory nationalists were outraged. They accused

Newtownabbey council of operating a sectarian policy. However, the council said it refused to name parks after anyone killed as a result of the Troubles. The Rathcoole branch of the UDA claimed two other young lives about the same time. 18 year-old Gavin Brett, a Protestant with a Catholic father, was sprayed with bullets from a passing car on the mixed Catholic Hightown Road, two miles from the Protestant Rathcoole estate. His killers mistook him for a Catholic, simply because he was standing in a Catholic area. His father, a paramedic, was called to attend the scene of his own son's murder, just yards from the family home. When he arrived Gavin was dying at the roadside.

In August 2002 the UDA struck again. This time they killed 19 year-old Gerard Lawlor as he walked along the Whitewell road itself. Gunmen on a motorbike drew alongside him as he walked home alone. He died instantly, just yards from the family home.

Much of the paramilitary activity at the time also had its roots in a wider loyalist feud in Belfast which more or less ended at the start 2003 when Johnny Adair's faction was forced to leave their Lower Shankill stronghold after he had ordered the killing of another UDA brigadier, John Gregg.

The sectarian tensions in the Whitewell allowed loyalist paramilitaries to gain dominance by shooting Catholics. According to Sinn Féin's Danny Lavery, a councillor for the area, the murders struck not only fear but anger in the local Catholic community.

"These three were all young people gunned down by the UDA and other teenagers could identify with them. Catholics were under attack not just in our homes and in our own streets but as we walked down the road from a night in the pub or stood chatting to friends on the street. It definitely made people wary about where they walked, although that has always been the case, but it also made people angry that this was happening and no-one seemed to give a damn."

In response to the trouble and the rising level of sectarian murders high-tech CCTV cameras were installed on the Whitewell Road. The PSNI said it would help identify persistent rioters and deter troublemakers. Loyalist community workers embraced the move with gusto. They said it would help tell the world the true story of who was starting the trouble. Eddie McClean, a loyalist community worker with a paramilitary record, even toured Protestant areas showing school children how effective the cameras were.

"It really did the trick, they couldn't believe how accurate these things were and it put the fear of God into them," he explained.

However nationalists took a different view of the cameras. To the Whitewell community it was a lame response to a concerted loyalist effort to kill and intimidate them.

The Marching Season plays an important part in raising sectarian tensions in the area. Since 1998 the Orange Order has been banned from marching past nationalist houses on the Whitewell Road. This is a cause of deep resentment to the local Protestant community, who view it as their right to parade along the road. Equally local republicans are banned from parading along part of the Whitewell interface. The Whitewell area is just over a mile from Glengormley, a village on the outskirts of north Belfast. Many Whitewell Catholics attend St Bernard's Church in the town and bury loved ones in the adjoining Carnmoney Cemetery.

In June 2001 the church was destroyed in an arson attack thought to be carried out by extreme loyalists. Less than a month later Catholic families attending cemetery Sunday, an annual outdoor mass held for the souls of the dead, were picketed by loyalists from Rathcoole and White City. It was a scene eerily reminiscent of the Harryville protests at Ballymena (see later), which ended in 1999. The police and British Army had to stop the protesters invading the cemetery and riots broke out later. St Bernard's Parish Priest, Fr Dan Whyte, said he had never witnessed scenes like it and took the unusual step of issuing public statements calling for anti-Catholic sectarianism to be addressed.

"It is deeply worrying and at the time I was very afraid for the wellbeing of my parishioners. There are good people on all sides of the community but it seemed that Catholics in Glengormley were being targeted and nothing was being done about it."

Fr Whyte contacted the office of the Police Ombudsman asking it to investigate the PSNI's lack of progress in catching the arsonists who destroyed his church. Since then he says things have improved for Catholics in the Whitewell and Glengormley areas. However, the arson attack promoted a series of copycat attacks on Protestant churches in the area. Carnmoney Presbyterian Church was almost destroyed when petrol was poured through a broken window. For a time it appeared that Glengormley was caught in a cycle of sectarian violence, most of it concentrated in Whitewell and White City.

As in most interface areas the issue of access to facilities plays a large part in maintaining simmering tensions. The largest civic amenity in the area is the Valley Leisure Centre near the loyalist Rathcoole estate. While Catholics complain it is out of bounds for them White City Protestants point out that to get to it they have to drive through Catholic areas.

Although the Whitewell trouble spread it was located mainly within a 100 yard radius, which made it less newsworthy and less likely to be addressed. The nearby Glengormley village has undergone significant demographic change over the past 15 years. Once a predominantly loyalist area it now has a significant Catholic community and in the last council elections held in Northern Ireland it elected its first Sinn Féin councillor, Briege Meehan.

A Protestant Glengormley spokesman, who requested anonymity for personal safety reasons, comments;

"What we are experiencing here is a countdown to a new violent interface. It's part of a strategy, cynically orchestrated by IRA/Sinn Féin, to create fresh community flash points across Northern Ireland and to create a pretext to abolish the symbols of the British tradition, including banning of Orange Parades, due to spurious claims that they are contentious.

"The growing electoral mandate of the SDLP and Sinn Féin councillors has given those representatives an arrogance which places political objectives above cross-community harmony.

"Elmfield, a 1960's estate of modern owner-occupied houses, is now virtually a Catholic ghetto. Protestant families living in a chill-factor environment, have moved out. Their homes when put on the market, attract only Catholics.

"The upper Hightown Road area, with its expanding housing development, has acquired a reputation as a future Catholic area, albeit, a middle class one. Protestant interest in purchasing a house there has declined. The proximity of a nearby Catholic school on the Hightown Road, acts as a focus for continuing one-community growth. In the past two years, Sinn Féin have objected to the ceremonial Orange Arch erected over the main street – a tradition each July going back over many years without disputes. However, the court cases brought by Sinn Féin were rejected as groundless. Other objections and violence have been directed against Orange Parades going past 'nationalist' areas, such as Elmfield, which is no-where near a Parade route.

"Such political, sectarian stirring-up by Catholic ex-tremists, does not bode well for the stable, happy cross-community I wish for my family."

●●●●●●●●

It is obvious from the contributors to this chapter that this interface situation is seen very differently indeed by the two communities. Such are the degrees of sus-picion that every development, political or demo-graphic, is often assumed to be have been manipu-lated by "the other side".

Many observers suggest that this is symptomatic of a lack of continuous dialogue. Those on the ground contend that they have "tried talking". Whatever hap-pens next, both communities will be watching politi-cal developments (the coming elections and possi-ble creation of a new Executive) with interest.

Chapter 3
North and West Belfast, Tigers Bay, Newington, the New Lodge and the Springfield Road

North Belfast is often described as a patchwork quilt of sectarian ghettoes. Staunchly loyalist neighbourhoods sit side-by-side with republican areas in what has become known as the killing fields of north Belfast. The area has in many ways been a microcosm of the Troubles in Northern Ireland, a third of all Catholics killed during the conflict having been murdered there. The security forces and Protestants also suffered heavy losses in the area at the hands of the IRA.

Catholics and Protestants live cheek by jowl in the heartland of north Belfast and most of the peace lines have been built there. The Shankill Butchers, a UVF gang which abducted and tortured their Catholics victims before killing them, operated almost exclusively in north Belfast. Despite the area's bloody history the 1994 ceasefires seemed to offer a chance of peace for its Protestant and Catholic communities.

Unlike many other areas the peace lines in north Belfast predate the 1994 ceasefires but since then a number of new ones have been erected as a response to sectarian violence. Between June and October 1996 north Belfast suffered extensive and widespread sectarian violence as a result of both the Drumcree crisis and the Orange Order's Tour of the North which takes it past many flashpoint areas. In the three months of trouble that followed at least 110 families, both Catholic and Protestant, had to leave their homes because of sectarian intimidation. Many people felt it was the worst sectarian violence they had experienced since the early days of the Troubles.

New peace lines were built or extended at the Whitewell, Duncairn Gardens, Newington and Alliance Avenue. Although the peace lines were built to stop trouble many believe they have only had a limited success. Indeed the presence of a barrier earmarks the boundary and may attract rioters from outside the area.

Manor Street, just off the Cliftonville Road in north Belfast, once dubbed 'murder mile', has had a peace line since the late 1980's. The barrier divides the street into Catholic and Protestant quadrants, however during the 1980's and 1990's gunmen regularly shot over the security fence at Catholic homes.

The barriers themselves can also reinforce a sense

of territoriality. Division is so deep-rooted in north Belfast that a study carried out by Dr Brendan Murtagh of Queen's University Belfast found that, "different sets of estate agents, developers, and solicitors can, in some cases, serve almost self-contained systems, thus producing and reproducing segregation in the housing market."

The development of peace lines in north Belfast has also created wastelands which would otherwise be used to build public sector housing. This has created a housing crisis, particularly in working-class nationalist areas which are characterised by overcrowding and lack of space, in short they are bursting at the seams, while houses in nearby Protestant areas lie empty. According to the 2001 census Catholic areas have higher than average family sizes and a more youthful demographic structure. Of the 1,701 families on the north Belfast housing waiting list, 1,276 are Catholic.

The solution may seem obvious but in the fenced-off world that is north Belfast nothing is simple. The peace lines may represent a degree of safety to the people who live on either side of them but they are also metal barriers which prevent movement from one community to the other. Nationalists say the peace lines act to hem in their expanding community in north Belfast, while Unionists, whose numbers are in decline in north Belfast, prefer to see them as a necessary fact of life, which provide some element of security. According to Housing Executive statistics, the body responsible for providing social housing in Northern Ireland, the highest incidence of segregated housing estates is in Belfast. Their research showed that almost 100% of public housing estates in Belfast are segregated. The Housing Executive regards an area as segregated if it contains less than 10% of the opposite religion.

Segregation has always been a feature of life in Belfast. At the start of the Troubles makeshift barricades were erected to stop incursions. These were particularly important at the start of the Troubles. In some cases, such as that of Bombay Street, whole streets were burned to the ground and their residents were forced to flee. Gradually, however, these gave way to permanent peace lines.

Sadly, not a single peace line erected in any part of Belfast has ever been taken down and with approximately 25 interface areas in north Belfast, this has lead to a burgeoning of such walls.

According to a report published by the north Belfast Community Development Centre, an organisation established in 1994 and which works with both Catholics and Protestants, a number of factors play a key role in underpinning the violence that occurs in interface communities.

The 1999 report found that poor communication between interface communities, especially during the worst periods of trouble, the role played by young people engaged in 'rioting for fun' and the role of paramilitary and political leaders helped prolong and intensify the trouble.

It was also shown that the interface areas are more deprived than others in terms of facilities and had high levels of long-term unemployment. Continued interface violence, especially at Alliance Avenue and Glenbryn and the demands by the Protestant community for a gate across the Ardoyne Road also helped to keep segregation high on the local agenda. Not surprisingly some of the worst trouble in recent years has occurred at north Belfast's flashpoint areas. The trouble is especially bad during the summer marching season, but the recent violence has been so intense that even on Christmas Day 2001 shots were fired into the home of a young Catholic mother living opposite Tigers Bay.

One of the worst trouble spots has been at the interface between the loyalist Tigers Bay and the nationalist Newington and Parkside estate. All three areas meet at the Limestone Road. Tigers Bay also fronts on to North Queen Street, a road which links the area to the republican New Lodge Road. Since the start of 2000 until late 2002 trouble flared there almost continuously. Tigers Bay is a small, dwindling loyalist estate, which has seen a steady decline in its population over the past 20 years, now with many elderly residents. It is reflective of many Protestant working-class areas in north Belfast which have experienced similar population decline in recent years.

New Lodge itself once had a significant Protestant community. But the upsurge in Troubles violence following internment in 1971, together with the intimidation many residents say they experienced, forced Protestants to abandon their homes.

Tiger Bay's population is an aging one with most young families living there as only a stopgap measure. Many north Belfast Protestants now prefer to live on the outskirts in places such as Carrickfergus which provides better quality housing at more affordable prices. Many of the houses in Tigers Bay still lie derelict, despite a replacement scheme in the area which took place nearly ten years ago, a source of resentment to Catholics.

The proximity of the nationalist New Lodge across the road, deters Protestant couples from taking-up these houses, due to fear and insecurity caused by attacks.

Youths from the area regularly riot with their nationalist neighbours in Parkside, Newington and Duncairn Gardens. Because of the riots a new peace line was built to separate Newington from Tigers Bay and a new security gate was erected where Tigers Bay meets Duncairn Gardens. A bank of eight high-tech CCTV cameras, directly linked to police headquarters, were installed on the Limestone Road as a security response to the violence. However trouble continued and the nightly clashes claimed their first victim when Protestant teenager, Glenn Brannagh, died when a pipe bomb he was holding exploded during a riot. The 16 year-old from Tigers Bay was a member of the UDA's youth wing.

Tigers Bay was once a thriving community until the onset of the Troubles. The reason for its decline lies in various socioeconomic factors such as the loss of heavy industry in the area. Economic factors, however, do not give the full picture. Like most interface communities it is a simple fact that tensions are sometimes taken out during riots or stone-throwing. Eddie McClean is a former paramilitary prisoner with links to the UDA. During most of the time when the violence was at its peak the UDA was deemed to have broken its ceasefire.

Despite this he says the violence at the interfaces was at least equally the work of republicans. Like many Protestants in north Belfast he regards the trouble as primarily due to Catholic expansion in north Belfast.

"The people in Tigers Bay don't want Catholics to move into the area. We have problems of our own and it just isn't practical to start moving Catholics into here. This community is deprived enough as it is and all the people are fighting for is to stay together as a community. Republicans started the trouble in a lot of the cases, I'm not saying our people didn't start it some of the time but it was much less often than the papers made out. You only have to look at the Catholic community to see why the trouble would come from their side. For a start the IRA want to keep their hard-liners on side and second they want more space to move into, but that isn't going to happen. There are other areas of Belfast they can go to, we don't want them here."

Eddie also believes that Catholics on the housing waiting list have been shipped in from other areas to massage the figures.

"They want to make north Belfast green just like it is in West Belfast so that is why they are shipping people in, to redraw the electoral map."

The view may seem paranoid but it is one shared by many working-class Protestants in north Belfast. However this perspective appears to be contradicted by several facts.

The PSNI's Assistant Commander for north Belfast said in July 2002 that the UDA in Tigers bay was responsible for most of the trouble at the interface. In a hard-hitting statement he said the UDA seemed incapable of living in peace with their Catholic neighbours.

Fear and mutual distrust are common at interfaces and their effects are wide reaching. In research carried out by Dr Pete Shirlow it was found that one third of residents had experienced physical and verbal violence in their local areas. Eighty-nine percent of Catholics and 79% of Protestants felt scared to cross into the other's area during the day. That figure rose to almost 100% after dark. It is widely believed by nationalists that much of the violence in north Belfast has been orchestrated by the UDA in order to reinforce its standing within its own community, in much the same way as the republican groupings would claim to be protecting their own community.

The human cost of the violence at the Tigers Bay interface with Newington and Parkside has been immense. Many houses bear the scars of petrol bombs, bullets and blast bombs. Newington Avenue which once won the best kept street in Belfast Award was on the receiving end of most of the attacks. In July 2002 the street's residents clubbed in to buy hard-hats for their children to protect against bricks and bottles when they were playing outside In the summer of 2002 a peace line was erected there to protect the houses which back onto Tigers Bay.

Marie Quigley lives in Newington Street with her family. A native of Co. Clare in the Republic of Ireland she describes the interface violence that erupted two years ago as the most frightening ordeal of her life.

"We couldn't use the back of the house because the loyalists were throwing stones over day and night. We had paint bombs, petrol bombs, and pipe bombs, everything thrown at the house. At night-time we couldn't sleep because the house was getting pelted and I was just living on my nerves. The children were terrified of going to sleep and being burned to death by a petrol bomb, so we had to sit up at night time and take turns to keep guard. I had never experienced anything like it in my life."

As the trouble threatened to drag on past the summer a series of secret talks between Sinn Féin, the

Ulster Unionist Party and community workers from Tigers Bay were held at Stormont. The talks were aimed at putting a stop put to the trouble but they still lasted for several weeks.

One of those who took part was senior Sinn Féin member Gerry Kelly. He said any chance the talks had of stopping violence at the interface were scuppered by UDA demands to end the trouble before talks could continue.

"We explained that the trouble was more than likely going to flare up and that was no reason for ending the talks. The whole idea was to keep the talks going because while the talks are ongoing there is more chance of finding a resolution. I was very disappointed when they were called off after a few weeks."

Tigers Bay didn't suffer a population shift during the trouble because most of the houses on the loyalist side of the interface were already vacated. In the small nationalist Parkside area, which lies directly opposite Tigers Bay, all but one of the residents moved out. Donna McDaid applied to be moved, but because of a housing shortage was forced to stay throughout the worst of the trouble.

The trouble in north Belfast which centred around Tigers Bay and the surrounding nationalist areas became so bad that siren systems were installed to alert residents of riots. At the sounds of the sirens residents, mostly young men, raced to the scene of the trouble. Often violence would break out on the Limestone Road and Duncairn Gardens simultaneously.

During the summer riots on the Limestone Road were daily and nightly occurrences, this being partly due to the tensions associated with the marching season. However the parades disputes themselves are seen by some as much a product of the sectarian division of territory as a factor reinforcing it. A peace line was erected at Duncairn Gardens in the 1990's, stretching for about 100 metres and seals off the New Lodge from Tigers Bay.

The bottom half of it is dominated by business centres which effectively act as another buffer zone between the two communities. Although the centres were built at a cost of millions they lay empty for many years. Research has shown that few industries or business are based in interface areas, due to obvious problems. The only multinational company which the Duncairn Business Park did eventually attract, Tele-Tech, threatened to pull-out in 2002 because of the sustained rioting.

Gerard Brophy is a Sinn Féin councillor from the area and spent most of the time on the streets during the trouble. He believes the tensions were worse than at any point during the Troubles.

"I am from the New Lodge myself and I never experienced that level of rioting even during the 1970's. It was nonstop and it has left behind a host of problems in its wake. People are more entrenched than ever before and from the point of view of the nationalist community we are less likely to have space for new housing. The peace lines have been reinforced because of the trouble and that means land which could have been used for housing will be wasted. The New Lodge is already bursting at the seams, so the problem will just be worse in five or ten years time. It means more houses will have to be built in the New Lodge itself, where there is no space left, so effectively it is ghettoising the community."

A row of newly-built Catholic houses at the junction of Duncairn Gardens were attacked so regularly that a wire-mesh grill was constructed at the front of them. Residents are no longer able to access their houses through their front-doors, instead having to use an alleyway.

The riots also led to a row over access to amenities. The Doctor's surgery used by Catholics from the New Lodge is located on the Protestant side of the road. On a number of occasions Catholics using the surgery were attacked by Protestants. In one instance a mini-siege developed when a Catholic teenager was trapped inside as her family tried to rescue her.

The problem of access to public facilities at Duncairn Gardens is one common to nearly all interface communities. Resources such as medical centres and post offices may be just yards up the road but if they lie in the 'other side's' territory they are deemed off-limits. That means crossing to a shop on the wrong side or taking a ten-minute detour to another can be a big decision.

The lack of resources for interface communities also

adds to the frequency of rioting. The marching season coincides with school holidays and many young people are faced with a long summer with nothing to do. In that scenario rioting with the opposite religion can seem an exciting alternative.

Community workers and politicians from both sides of the divide agree that more resources need to be given to interface areas. Research by the Belfast Interface Project in 1998 based on interviews with interface residents found a severe lack of facilities in these areas. The conditions have led to what has been dubbed 'recreational rioting' by teenagers. The fragile and poor relationships between the co-existing communities can also mean that a minor incident such as stone-throwing by a small group of teenagers can lead to a full-scale riot. In a bid to counter this, and in the wake of the 1996 riots at north Belfast interfaces, a mobile phone network was established between Protestant and Catholic community workers.

Although the network has been successful in stopping riots before they start its success depends on the willingness of community workers from both sides to use it. Sometimes there have been complaints that phones have been switched off during riots or that community workers have said they can do nothing to stop them. Ironically young people on both sides of the divide were accused of ringing another to start riots, via mobile phones.

Fred Cobain is the UUP Assembly member for north

Belfast and a member of the newly-formed Policing Boards. He says that there has been little strategic planning developed to counteract the patterns that interface communities fall into.

"Unless you do this in a strategic way it won't work, and the only way you can tackle them is over a long protracted period of time and state agencies are needed. There has been no real strategic investment so far. The rise in tensions can be put down to the fact that loyalists and republicans used interface areas as a way of bolstering their own image in the community. For Unionists it was out of frustration with the political process. A lot of people in loyalist areas had no relationship with the police. In all there was very little community relations work done in the areas."

Fred Cobain describes Catholics moving into loyalist areas "a red flag to a bull."

"That just won't happen, the paramilitaries in the loyalist areas just won't allow it. It will just move the interfaces forward, it is like pouring petrol on the fire. Protestant communities would see it as an invasion; people in these interfaces blame the other party, taking down the walls is going to make that worse not better."

However he describes the talks with Gerry Kelly as useful.

"Talks were useful. At least then we were all talking but I don't want to get into the blame game about who or what made them fail. Blame lies on both sides.

I've been on the interfaces and I've seen both sides involved in violence."

When riots spread to North Queen Street it meant people from the New Lodge and Tigers Bay who weren't directly affected became involved giving those involved a greater sense of community. Gunmen were posted on both sides at night to stop incursions, something which actually had been happening on and off from the early 1970's.

Sometimes what happens takes on an absurd quality. The scourge of joyriding, where disaffected youths steal cars and drive them at high speed along the road at night, has been a growing problem and community workers and even sometimes the IRA have been called on to bring an end to it. The practice has claimed many innocent lives in Catholic areas of the city, mostly in the west. In July 2002 a Catholic joyrider deliberately knocked down and killed a Protestant man standing on the Protestant side of the road. This obviously sectarian attack sparked great anger amongst the Protestant community and even though the IRA expelled those involved from the country it did little to quell the reaction.

Another example of how ludicrous what happens along the peace lines must seem to the outsider is Alexandra Park in north Belfast. The park itself has a peace line built right through it having been built in the 1990's to stop daily riots between rival Catholic and Protestant youths. The park has virtually stopped being used as a recreational amenity and has succumbed to the civil pressures around it. It seems that north Belfast's long history of sectarian killings and strife, dating back to the 1920's, could continue for some time.

West Belfast, on the other hand is less a patchwork of rival communities living cheek by jowl, though this does not mean that the problems faced here are any less protracted. The area is predominantly nationalist with a large loyalist community on the Shankill Road which serves as a link with other large loyalist areas in north Belfast. The peace line in west Belfast stretches practically from Castle Street, in the city centre at the bottom of the Falls Road, certainly from Divis Street, Percy Street, Dover Street, right up the road.

The Springfield Road is one of the crossover points between nationalist and loyalist west Belfast, one of the few entry points along an area characterised by large walls separating the two communities. This area has seen some of the worst violence, particularly during the marching season when members of the Loyal Orders demanded to march along the nationalist part of the road.

Serious trouble often broke out with residents claiming that loyalist paramilitary banners were openly on show during these marches, this at a time when there was an organised campaign of sectarian murder being carried out against Catholics in the area. Over the last few years the Parades Commission has permitted loyalist marches in this area while putting restrictions on the marches themselves, although these have not been strictly observed.

The area's MP, Gerry Adams sees the problem in historic terms.

"If you look at the history of the area particularly around Divis Street and the lower part of the Springfield they have been sites of sectarian clashes going back over 150 years, probably even longer."

He also sees the peace walls as an indication of a failed policy on the part of the government.

"The problem with the peace wall is it almost institutionalises the division and I am speaking as someone who had to lobby for them not only to be built, but at times for them to be raised because of incursions by loyalists. It is a very sad indictment of the state. They have become permanent structures. People built barricades for protection and defence but they never envisaged they would have this division permanently. The security bases weren't meant to stop the sectarian violence, the reality was that the British Army see nationalists as the enemy community and so they weren't interested in protecting Catholics. Obviously on the surface anyway, not for any reasons of endearment, the British Army has worked on the basis that you can't fight two enemies at once."

Politics also has an impact on the dynamic of the situation, according to Adams, particularly the DUP's refusal to speak to Sinn Féin.

"If Catholics are stigmatised at a community level, if we are terrorised, then you can't blame youngsters if they replicate the behaviour of their political 'leaders'."

The local people have taken steps to try to tackle problems in this area and the Springfield Intercom Development Project encourages both sides to defuse problems before they become insurmountable. A network of mobile phones has been established to give prior warning to trouble brewing, for example. The nationalists on Springfield Road also made a series of proposals to the Orange Order in 2003, prior to its march along the road, and although the Order refused to acknowledge these, there was no trouble at what for years before had been a flashpoint.

However, Protestant confidence in cross-community forums received a serious setback last year when the police recovered the personal details of Protestant Community workers during the search of a suspected republican's house. Most Protestants withdrew from the forums as a result, on personal safety grounds.

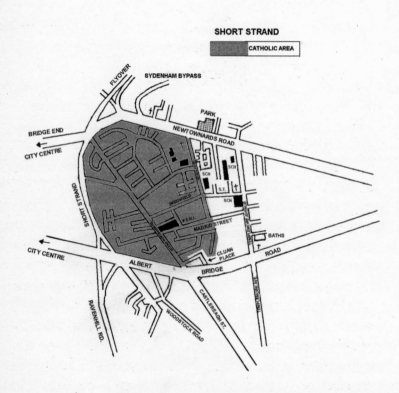

The area to the west of Short Strand bounded by the River Lagan and city centre approaches is neutral territory.

Chapter 4
Short Strand

The first barrier ever built to separate Catholics and Protestants was erected in the Short Strand area of East Belfast in 1920. A tiny nationalist enclave of some 3,000 people it sits in the overwhelmingly Protestant East Belfast, which has a population of around 60,000. A speck of green in a sea of orange, its importance in the nationalist psyche of the North cannot be overestimated. For it was here that the Provisional IRA cemented their position as defenders of their community. In June 1970 three IRA gunmen used a sniping perch in the grounds of the Short Strand's St Matthew's Catholic Church to defend the area from a mob of loyalists. Three loyalists and one IRA man died in the gun battle which bolstered the IRA's role as not only defenders of the Short Strand but, of all northern nationalists.

Protestants regard the area with suspicion and hostility and as a hotbed of republican activity. The Newtownards Road and Woodstock Road, both hard-line loyalist areas, surround the Short Strand. The area is partially enclosed by a 40-foot high peace line and security gates, prompting some residents to describe it as an 'open prison.'

In the past 40 years, extensive redevelopment in Short Strand, Lower Newtownards Road and Woodstock Road, has shrunk both communities by 60%. Despite a lower population, sporadic sectarian attacks by both sides has been endemic in the area, especially since 1969.

In one incident on April 12 1975 a UVF bomb killed six people in a bar in the Short Strand. The Strand Bar bombing was one of many random sectarian attacks carried out by loyalists on the area during the Troubles.

In an earlier incident an explosion in a house killed several people and was assumed at first to be a loyalist attack. However, it transpired that the explosion was the result of a tragic IRA 'own goal' by one of its bomb-makers.

Whatever the causes, such incidents only heightened the tension between both communities.

In the summer of 2002 the Short Strand was once again in the front-line of sectarian violence. For more than six months large-scale riots between Catholics, Protestants, the PSNI and the British Army were a nightly occurrence. Dozens of houses on each side were destroyed and residents were forced to move from their homes. In the Short Strand houses were set on fire by petrol-bombers and residents were forced to cover their windows and doors with plywood. In the tiny loyalist enclave of Cluan Place, nearly all the houses were vacated and residents daubed 'Welcome to Hell' on the walls.

The inter-communal violence which broke out in the Short Strand/Cluan Place interface was perhaps the most violent and dangerous of all the trouble in Belfast over the summer of 2002. With the memories of 1970 still alive nationalists in the Short Strand lived with the continual fear that their area might be overran at any minute and their homes destroyed.

According to nationalists the recent trouble began on May 11 2002 when a crowd of loyalists gathered at the Madrid Street interface and attacked Catholic owned homes. Five blast-bombs were thrown from the loyalist side. They say loyalists started the attacks in a bid to force the NIO to build an extra security gate on to the Short Strand and to try and force the IRA to break its ceasefire and thus collapse the peace process. Loyalists deny that, saying that the violence started because Catholics repeatedly attacked Protestant homes in Cluan Place. They also claim that republicans broke promises given to them in private meetings aimed at averting trouble.

The violence lasted for six months before it was brought under control, but the area was still prone to sporadic violence months afterwards. By the time the trouble ended more than 100 pipe bombs had been thrown at Catholic houses, and republican gunmen had shot five Protestants.

Physically the most permanent result of the trouble is a new security gate erected at the Madrid Street/Thistle Court interface, leaving the Short Strand almost entirely fenced in on two sides by barriers of one sort or another. During the worst of the trouble Short Strand residents nearest the front line lived with buckets of water by their doors in case of petrol bomb attack and nearly every house had grills or wooden boards on it.

The nearest doctor's surgery, chemist and post office, which people from the Short Strand could access, were in a loyalist area and loyalists told Catholics to stay away from them or risk being shot.

Although the trouble was broadcast on TV and the area was visited by the Secretary of State, John Reid, to those involved it seemed that the world sat and watched on. Joe O'Donnell is a Sinn Féin councillor for the Short Strand, the first nationalist ever to be elected in East Belfast. He says the violence of the Short Strand can only be understood as a siege.

"People could not get out of the area, we couldn't use vital facilities for weeks on end and there simply wasn't the political will to deal with it from the British Government and Unionist politicians. The area was like the Warsaw Ghetto, people were sleeping in relatives' houses and loyalists were attacking the area with impunity. The PSNI stood by and let them, in fact their only response was to stop our people from defending the area. They came into the Short Strand and raided houses, they fired plastic bullets and behaved like thugs. That is what we were up against for six months. During the daytime loyalists would play loud music from speakers in Cluan Place so that people in the Short Strand couldn't get to sleep and at night-time the attacks would begin again. People were living in houses that were totally boarded up to protect against the attacks. Effectively that meant people were living in houses with no light."

And Joe O'Donnell says the only people who profited from the violence were anti-agreement Unionists, despite publicly distancing themselves from the trouble.

"This trouble just didn't start from nowhere and for no reason, the loyalists who began attacking our homes did so with a blatant agenda in mind. Anyone who thinks people from the Short Strand wanted to take on East Belfast simply doesn't know what they are talking about. There are 3,000 people living here, does anyone think it is feasible that we wanted to take on the whole of East Belfast?"

Republicans like Joe O'Donnell believe loyalists started the trouble to destabilise the peace process and as part of a longer-term policy to 'box' the Short Strand in.

"The people who had the reasons for starting the trouble were the loyalists. First of all on a grassroots level they wanted a security gate erected at Madrid Street meaning our area is totally confined. They got their way in that regard. But on a wider level the aim of the violence was to try and force the IRA to break a cease-fire and give David Trimble the excuse of walking away from the Assembly without blame. The UVF and UDA thought that they could help wreck the Assembly by attacking the Short Strand."

Unionist politicians, however, contend that there are no attempts to hem the Catholic community in and point to the fact that the PSNI confirm that restrictions exist on only two sides.

The ferocity of the trouble took most people by surprise. Within days of the first attack the Short Strand community was in a state of high-alert. Pensioners and those living on the front-line were being moved out of their houses while the media recorded the goings-on. Attempts to end the trouble were overtaken by the scale of the violence. By the time it was over dozens of people had been seriously injured and today bullet marks pepper some of the walls in the Short Strand area.

As the nightly battles raged a procession of high-profile politicians streamed through the Short Strand. John Reid, then secretary-of-state, visited the Short Strand and Protestants living in Cluan Place. Delegations from the Irish Department of Foreign Affairs, the British Conservative Party and International Observers from the US all came to see the violence at first hand. Arriving in bullet-proof ministerial cars the politicians made unlikely visitors to the area.

However, despite the visits and promises of political intervention the trouble continued, and during August the situation worsened still further. Nightly incidents of violence were recorded on both sides. Masked men appeared on the streets and pipe bombs and bricks were thrown over the peace line until the early hours of the morning. The violence would often continue into the early hours of the morning, with families forced to stay awake until the violence ended. Crowds of around 200 on each side were out on the streets, some armed with petrol bombs and cudgels.

Short Strand residents boarded up their houses, preferring to live in darkness than risk becoming the next victim of a pipe bomb attack.

Agnes McGinley, is a Catholic mother-of-two and nursery school teacher from the Short Strand. Her brother was killed in the Short Strand in 1972 and she says during the summer of 2002 people relied on local vigilantes for protection.

"They were the only ones who people trusted, they were out on the streets and they were looking after our interests. If it had have been left to the cops and the British Army the Short Strand would have been in flames, we would have burned out of here a long time ago. Most of the kids were too young to really know what was happening but sometimes they would ask what the explosions were the night before. The depths of the violence shocked me, we had toasters, pots of jam, tea, cups, all sorts thrown at us from loyalists in

Cluan Place. But what worried me was my own son's attitude. After the trouble had been going on for a while he became a lot more resentful of Protestants."

The violence had an obvious effect on the Short Strand, it was after all a small community, but also on the Protestant cul-de-sac of Cluan Place, which faces onto Clandeboye Street in the Short Strand. A distance of forty feet separates the two streets, with a 30-foot high wall in between.

It was mostly pensioners who lived in Cluan Place at the time of the violence. A street of just 24 houses it was completely empty within weeks of the trouble starting. Today eight families have moved back into the street.

Protestants accused people in the Short Strand of setting out to 'ethnically cleanse' the street and said the empty houses were proof of their claim that republicans wanted to take over Protestant houses. It has to be said that no Catholics have ever moved into these houses. When a Protestant family did move back into Cluan Place, the story made the local newspapers.

David Trimble visited Cluan Place to tell the media that Protestants were under a vicious assault by republicans and said Sinn Féin had questions to answer about its involvement in the attacks. One incident, which sparked Unionist calls for the IRA ceasefire to be declared void, came in August when five Protestant men were shot and injured by republican gunmen operating from the Short Strand area. Unionists cited it as proof that the IRA was in breach of its ceasefire and that the true aggressors were republicans. However national-ists in the Short Strand claimed that gunmen opened fire when a 100 strong gang of loyalists tried to breach the peace line at Cluan Place.

The MP for East Belfast, DUP Deputy Leader, Peter Robinson, caused further controversy when a booklet he produced on the violence ignored all loyalist vio-lence against the Short Strand. Cataloguing a series of incidents against Protestants Peter Robinson was lam-basted for ignoring the attacks on Catholic homes. Joe O'Donnell says that Peter Robinson failed in his duty as the area's MP to deal evenhandedly with the problem.

"His approach made the situation a lot worse. He refused to talk to the residents and he simply white-washed the fact that loyalists were shooting into peo-ple's houses and petrol bombing us every night. It was a godsend to the UDA and UVF who were under no political pressure to stop from within their own com-munity. It confirmed what people in the Short Strand have always known, that the rest of East Belfast doesn't want us."

One of the key figures on the loyalist side who tried to find a resolution to the dispute was the Progressive Unionist Party's (PUP) David Ervine. Ironically he had been involved in talks with Sinn Féin and community workers on both sides of the divide in the weeks lead-ing up to the trouble. However when the trouble be-gan he refused to talk to Sinn Féin saying there was little point in negotiating.

He claims that on 11 May an agreement had been reached between republicans and the UDA and UVF that no paramilitary organisation would start trouble at the Short Strand/Cluan Place interface. The agreement came after face-to-face talks at Church Hall in Glengall Street, supervised by Protestant cleric Gary Mason. David Ervine says that when trouble did break out the next day he felt "shafted."

"We had been engaged in talks for a few weeks before the serious trouble began, to try and make sure there was no violence. Those talks included me and Joe O'Donnell among others and, we all agreed that we would ask the main paramilitary groups not to engage in violence. We each agreed to see that the UVF, IRA and UDA would sign up to not being involved in the interface violence. About two weeks later we got everyone on board to run this system and then the next night all hell broke loose. A crowd of nationalists were attacking houses at the Madrid Street interface, after that I thought there was little point in talking to Sinn Féin. It was clear that a decision had been taken to attack the houses and no matter what they said to you it was a question of the trust having broken down. They virtually invaded Madrid Street and people were afraid for their lives, they just swept by PSNI Land Rovers and attacked the houses with whatever they could get their hands on."

Joe O'Donnell rejects those claims, however. He says the UVF threw five blast bombs into the Short Strand the next night without any provocation. But David Ervine also states that despite media reports claiming the UDA were behind the violence in Cluan Place, it was in fact the UVF.

"I have to give credit where it is due and say the UDA tried very hard to keep their people out of the trouble. The UVF was behind the violence there, they saw themselves as protecting the community. There is no point in me telling lies and saying that it wasn't the UVF, it was. But it was a response to the republican violence that was threatening innocent Protestant lives. If people hadn't responded the area would have been overrun. The Provos were interested in starting the violence for two reasons. Firstly they were coming under pressure from people within their own community and secondly they were resentful of the peace lines around them. Ironically there would have been no gate erected at Madrid street if it hadn't have been for the violence of last year."

David Ervine is a representative for the PUP, the political party which gives advice to the UVF, a fact which gives further credibility to the above statement.

Clearly there has been little trust on either side since the trouble began. David Ervine says that the IRA's refusal to acknowledge its involvement in the trouble has left Unionists with little or no confidence when talking to republicans. However he argues that trust is not essential for peace.

"We don't trust each other, a lot of people don't trust

each other but that doesn't mean we have to try and kill one another. If we agree to leave one another alone then that is the best thing. People on the loyalist side of the peace line would see the Short Strand as being controlled by the IRA and at the same time they would see the IRA as being out and out liars. The IRA lies really annoyed people and it means that there is no enthusiasm to get into fresh dialogue, but then the reality is that without dialogue of some sort we don't have much to go on. But I took a lot of stick from people on my own side of the fence for being too soft on Sinn Féin."

East Belfast UUP councillor Jim Rogers is a former Lord Mayor of Belfast. During the trouble he talked to Joe O'Donnell and other Belfast republicans in an effort to get the trouble stopped. However he says republicans are responsible for starting the trouble. Like many Unionists in other interface areas of Belfast he sees the trouble's roots in republican territorial ambition.

"The trouble was clearly planned by Sinn Féin and the IRA, they wanted more houses for their people to move into and the only way they were going to get them was by intimidating people out of Cluan Place. The trouble set community relations back years - there is distrust among Protestants of people from the Short Strand."

Michael Copeland is a UUP councillor for the Borough of Castlereagh. During the summer of 2002 he spent virtually every night in Cluan Place and eventually adopted a child from the area. He says that the media has ignored the plight of Protestants in the area. Like most Unionists he sees the street violence there as a result of Catholics trying to move in.

"How republicans can sit and say that the trouble in the Short Strand was orchestrated by loyalists is just beyond me. It is a load of rubbish, the people who lived in Cluan Place were pensioners, and they weren't out throwing stones and petrol bombs. These people were forced out of their houses by the actions of militant republicans who then tried to portray themselves as the victims. By the end of the trouble Cluan Place was like a ghost-town, people simply couldn't live there anymore, whereas if you look at the Short Strand today there are no empty houses. It is no secret that the Short Strand community is an expanding one and they want to continue that expansion by moving into new houses. The easiest way to do that is to get the likes of Cluan Place, force the people to move out and then take the houses for themselves. It was sectarian in its nature, they didn't want Protestants to live there so they thought they would get them out in the most effective way possible, intimidation. This is what the trouble is all about."

The Short Strand violence came at a time when sectarian tensions were at their highest in Belfast for many years. In north Belfast riots were a daily happening on interface areas such as the Limestone Road, North Queen Street and the Ardoyne Road. The UDA was no longer on ceasefire and senior members of the PSNI accused the UDA of deliberately provoking trouble at interface areas. However Michael Copeland is adamant that the Short Strand trouble could have been avoided if republicans hadn't been intent on taking over Protestant homes.

"No-one in Cluan Place or indeed in East Belfast wanted the trouble. It has had a very negative impact on the whole community here and it is an experience that people do not want to see repeated."

One major bone of contention for both nationalists and loyalists was the role played by the PSNI and British Army. Both sides accused the security forces of heavy-handedness in tackling the problem. However in the Short Strand resentment at the behaviour of the PSNI and British Army is much more acute. On May 14, three days after the trouble began, the PSNI and military sealed off the Short Strand in a raid for weapons. Nationalists not only saw the raid as provocative but as lending legitimacy to the loyalist's claims that the trouble was originating in the Short Strand. Residents protested against the raids and within minutes the PSNI and British Army fired 16 plastic bullets into the crowd. An Irish News photographer and a 16 year-old boy were among those hit by the bullets. In the event nothing except for contraband cigarettes and an imitation gun were recovered. No arrests were made.

The violent and angry confrontation between members of the PSNI and Short Strand residents became a feature of the six-month long trouble. A constant theme in nationalists' attitudes to the PSNI and British Army is that both were more interested in containing a nationalist response to the loyalist violence than in stopping it. However Unionists demanded a heavier security force presence in the Short Strand.

Peter Robinson called for permanent PSNI and British Army checkpoints in the area and for house-to-house searches. The PUP's David Ervine said the PSNI were trying to curry favour with nationalists in a bid to get Sinn Féin to join the Policing Boards later that year. Nationalists accused the security forces of allowing loyalist to gather in Cluan Place. Joe O'Donnell says the PSNI could have easily prevented the crowds.

"Cluan Place is a cul-de-sac yet every night crowds of around 150 loyalists were able to gather there and throw stones at our houses. People were asking why the PSNI and British Army didn't prevent them from congregating there every night. It showed that we weren't going to get any protection and the only people we could rely on were ourselves."

Undoubtedly the street violence has led to a sharpening of attitudes among young people living in interface areas. According to studies carried out by Dr Pete Shirlow of the University of Ulster, sectarianism in Northern Ireland has increased over the past ten years. And sectarianism is prevalent even in preschool age children. Dr. Shirlow says that sectarian clashes such as that in the Short Strand are bound to set back the antisectarian agenda for years to come.

"What we are seeing is another generation of young people who are witnessing the same violence and the same bitterness that our fathers and mothers witnessed. They are sleeping in fear at night and experiencing sectarianism at first hand. After the 1994 ceasefires people expected there to be a lot more mobility between areas but that didn't happen to a great degree. Up until Drumcree 1996 there is some anecdotal evidence to suggest that Catholics moved into areas which were traditionally Protestant and Protestants visited shopping centres in Catholic areas and so on. But after July 1996 people moved out again and stopped visiting those areas. Catholics who had moved into Protestant areas moved out again and since then we have seen an increasing level of territoriality in Belfast and in other areas."

Pete Shirlow's studies have found that sectarianism is more common among the younger generation in the North than with older people.

"Older people can remember a time when tensions weren't quite as high and also tend to take a longer view of things, they recognise that there is good and bad on all sides. But younger people tend not to think in this way, they are more sectarian in attitude. They also tend to ape the paramilitaries who would have been active in their areas up until 1994. They see themselves as defenders of the community and because many of them would be too young too remember

Parent and police escort a pupil to Holy Cross Primary

Young nationalists 'flying the flag' in Ardoyne

Loyalists protesting in North Belfast

Protester in North Belfast

Young protester throws stone at policeman

Aftermath of North Belfast riot

Orange marchers at Drumcree

Short Strand interface: a sculpture mural on Albert Bridge Road spelling 'Hope'. The brass inscription read 'Tomorrow's Faces'. An art mural portraying the faces of 40 young people from two schools, Netherfield and St Mathew's primary schools, who participated in this art project in order to offer something positive to the communities around the interface. This art piece is their offering to help build better relationships between young and old in both communities.

the Troubles at their worst they also tend to have less fear of engaging in violence. They want to take on the role of defending their community and that takes the form of attacking the people on the other side of the interface."

Dr Shirlow says his studies have found a high-level of despondency within Unionist areas in contrast to optimism within nationalist communities.

"Protestants believe they have gained little from the peace process. They feel that for 70 years they have been told the state they created will stop existing and now they are closer than ever to this. Republicans have an ideology which promises them a better future so there is a higher level of optimism within that constituency."

Dr Shirlow also argues that the conflicts around interfaces are essentially about territory. He says that through work with community groups on both sides of the divide he perceives a lack of willingness from either side to see the problems for another perspective.

"Unionism doesn't have the capacity to move forward or to negotiate in the way that republicanism does. Unionists tend to reject the idea that they are sectarian, just as republicans do. Around 80 to 90% of people on both sides see problems as being the other side's fault. The plain truth is of course that there is sectarianism on both sides."

And although inter-communal violence has blighted communities like the Short Strand, Pete Shirlow says that inside those communities cross-community relations are not high on people's wish-lists. And most of the working-class communities affected by the violence feel as though the so-called peace dividend has passed them by.

"We talked to people in those areas and essentially what comes out of it was that issues such as drug-dealing, unemployment and joyriding are much higher on people's agenda than cross-community dialogue. That may sound surprising but it isn't when you consider how much these areas are affected by these issues. But the whole idea that a lot of cross-community dialogue goes on in Northern Ireland seems to be something of a fallacy when you start to dig deeper. What is fairly clear is that there isn't even a realisation among each community of the others' needs."

One especially vicious sectarian incident came one Wednesday morning in June 2002. A funeral mass for Jean O'Neill, a Catholic pensioner from the Short Strand, was attacked by loyalist protesters on the Newtownards Road. Stones, bottles and slates were hurled over the chapel fence onto the heads of mass-goers and grieving relatives. Mourners were trapped in the grounds of St Matthew's Chapel for almost an hour before the PSNI brought the situation under control. The incident illustrated the viciousness of the conflict.

Joanne Walsh is a 33 year-old Protestant mother of one who moved to the Short Strand in 1997 says that after the trouble she no longer supports the PSNI. She says the violence opened her eyes to the experience of life on the nationalist side of the wall.

"Before last summer I would never have thought the trouble could be one sided, but it was. The Short Strand was attacked by loyalists for no other reason than it was Catholics on the other side. My home was pelted with bricks and bottles and petrol bombs, we were doing nothing but because of where we lived loyalists thought it was alright to torture us. I also witnessed first hand how the PSNI treated people in the area, they are definitely a one-sided force who have no respect for Catholics whatsoever. I was brought up to support the police but I definitely wouldn't now, I am even afraid to visit my family because I am afraid my car registration would give away where I live. That shows how people in the Short Strand are forced to live. At the time I felt embarrassed to be a Protestant."

In the aftermath of the trouble the Short Strand community centre was turned into a makeshift trauma unit. Teams of trauma specialists from the South Eastern Health Trust were drafted in to deal with children and adults who had endured six months of violence. One of the lighter moments of the long summer months in the Short Strand came when Irish folk legend Christy Moore gave a free concert for the community. Some families from the Short Strand were also offered holidays in the south of Ireland, staying with their hosts for free.

Brendan Bradley heads up the Survivors of Trauma group which looks after families, friends and relatives of those bereaved through the Troubles. He says the trauma of inter-communal violence such as that suffered in Short Strand and other interface areas can take years to heal.

"The impact on the whole community can be quite traumatic, but especially on parents and children. Children can start bed-wetting, stopping wanting to go to school and become very withdrawn. They don't understand what is going on and the one place they have been taught that is safe, i.e. home, is no longer a safe place for them. It becomes a place that is dangerous, they can't sleep at night and of course that stress and trauma is also felt by the parents. One of the things we need to see are proper resources being given to communities that have been through an experience like this. Throughout the Troubles victims have always been forgotten and more or less ignored by the state, they just haven't given over the resources that are needed to deal with it. But we need to get this right if we are to start building a new future. We can't ignore the fact that a community has been under attack for a year or six months or whatever and just ask them to sweep it under the carpet. It wouldn't happen in a middle-class area and it wouldn't happen in England or in the south of Ireland so why are working-class communities in the North expected to take the brunt of the sectarian violence without getting any help?"

Other professional advisers on trauma impact disagree and claim that any adverse effects are usually short term, claiming that children's natural resilience is a self protective mechanism less evident in adults.

Since October 2002 trouble in the Short Strand has tailed off, however there are still sporadic incidents of stone-throwing and other violence. One outcome of the violence was the setting-up of an inter-community network between the Short Strand and the Protestant areas, which surround it. The network is comprised of a neighbourhood watch scheme on both sides of the interface to try and stop trouble before it begins, a mobile phone network which works as an early warning system when trouble does begin and a forum for local politicians to meet. So far only the first two stages have been implemented and neither has been fully tested.

But according to community workers on both sides of the divide the system looks promising. Although neither believes that the new network is either foolproof or a long-term guarantee for peace. An indication of how far the two communities have come was a press statement released by Joe O'Donnell from Sinn Féin in the spring of 2003, praising the work of his Unionist colleagues in keeping a lid on trouble.

Chapter 5

The Fountain, Derry/Londonderry

The small loyalist Fountain Estate on the west bank of Derry City resembles the last outpost of the British Empire. On one side the historic walls of Derry block it off from the nationalist streets that surround it, while the rest of the estate is encased by security lines built during the Troubles. Derry itself is a largely nationalist city, birthplace of the Civil Rights movement and just yards from the border with the Irish Republic.

Inside the Fountain, the turret of the old Derry women's jail stands as a reminder of the area's past. Now though it has a security-wall cutting through it. Like a bunker, the area's only youth club is built underground. Tattered Union Jacks and UDA flags fly from empty houses and street lampposts, a sullen reminder to the nationalists of Derry that loyalism still exists in the West Bank of the city.

The Fountain is home to just over 300 people, but until the mid-1970's it had a population of more than

3,000. Many of the houses in the Fountain are derelict or ramshackle and unemployment runs at around 70%. The Protestants who live there are among the last in the west bank of Derry, 300 people in a population of almost 60,000. The rest of the city's Protestants moved across the Craigavon Bridge and into the Waterside during the 1970's.

Today there is even talk amongst Unionists in the Waterside of setting up a separate council and a de facto separate Derry or Londonderry for themselves, although recent census returns have showed that even here the Protestant majority is under threat. The controversial proposal would effectively create two cities, a Catholic and a Protestant one.

Until the Anglo-Irish Agreement of 1985 the Fountain Estate had the feel of an Israeli settler camp on Palestinian land. The British Government gave it special status, affording it the same level of protection as Derry's Security Zone, which was designed to stop the IRA bombing commercial targets in the town centre. All cars leaving and entering the Fountain were searched by British soldiers and armed RUC men. British Army regiments were stationed in the Fountain Estate until 1985, at one stage there was an estimated one soldier for every five residents.

According to Protestant community workers and Unionist politicians the removal of the security ring around the estate damaged the confidence of the Fountain's residents. But for some the last bugle sounded for the

Fountain when hundreds of residents were moved from their homes in the early 1970's as part of a redevelopment plan. The idea was to renovate houses and move the original inhabitants back as soon as possible. But as the Troubles raged and the IRA campaign in the city intensified Protestants were reluctant to move back so instead they sought refuge in the Waterside.

Until 1969 the history of Derry had been one of domination by the minority unionists over the city's majority nationalist population. Even though nationalist outnumbered unionist by more than two to one Unionist gerrymandering meant a nationalist MP had not been returned for the city.

Bloody Sunday, when the British Army shot dead 13 unarmed nationalist civilians taking part in a civil rights march in Derry, led to a massive resurgence of the IRA in the city. Some Protestants feared Catholics would take revenge for 50 years of domination and discrimination. Almost overnight the realities which underpinned Derry society were swept away by the violence of the Troubles.

Today the Protestants living in the Fountain say they feel like their ancestors hundreds of years before them, under siege, uncertain and fearful of what the future holds. Sporadic petrol-bombing and stone throwing incidents by nationalist youths who sometimes attack the estate reinforce that fear. And Unionists accuse nationalist Derry of ignoring their plight.

Nationalists and republicans in Derry emphatically

reject these claims. They say that the accommodation reached by the Bogside residents and the Apprentice Boys, which allowed the Apprentice Boys to march through contentious parts of the town unopposed is proof of that. And they point to a power-sharing policy in Derry City Council which saw DUP councillor Mildred Garfield, a native of the Fountain Estate, elected as Lord Mayor in 2001 as proof of their commitment to offering a "warm house" for Protestants in the city.

When in the summer of 2002 Catholic youths began attacking the Fountain estate regularly with brick and petrol bombs claiming it was in response to attacks on Catholic areas such as the Short Strand, a community meeting was held in the Bogside. Attended by Sinn Féin, the SDLP and nationalist community workers the public meeting told those responsible that the attacks were unacceptable and wouldn't be tolerated. Vigilantes were deployed on the Catholic side of the interface to make sure no trouble began. But despite initiatives such as that Unionists still insist that republicans have made the West Bank of the city a no-go area for Protestants.

The DUP's Gregory Campbell is the MP for East Londonderry, a native of the city, he believes that unless there is a change in attitude by nationalists the Fountain has a very uncertain future.

"Protestants don't feel comfortable in Derry, it is as simple as that. They can't walk through the city centre without seeing crowds of youths in Celtic football tops or without hearing people playing Irish music outside bars. It is an atmosphere that makes Protestants feel uncomfortable and it has got worse over the years instead of getting better. We hear a lot from nationalists about what they are going to do to make Derry a better place for the Protestant population but they never take any action. Something practical needs to be done about it, instead of the nice sound-bites which seem to come from them all the time."

He admits that getting teenagers to stop wearing Celtic football tops would be a near impossible task. However Campbell, a strong opponent of the Good Friday Agreement, dismisses the election of Mildred Garfield as Mayor and the Apprentice Boys accommodation as a PR stunt by republicans.

"They realised that they needed to be seen to do something that would make them look like the nice guys. They wanted to show how good it would be if they were in control, I don't think too many people were fooled by that approach.

"For years they talked about what they would do and did nothing. Then when the peace process came they started this. The nationalists in Londonderry are simply being clever by doing things like this, they know they have nothing to lose by it. Unless something radical changes Protestants in Derry have an uncertain future."

Despite his cynicism regarding nationalist initiatives Gregory Campbell is unsure about what exactly could be done to allay Protestant fears in the city. Outside of the nationalist areas of Derry there are virtually no republican walls mural or tricolours. Inside the Fountain Estate itself the outlook is less bleak.

Community worker Willie Temple, an Orangeman and former chemist, says there is a gradual confidence coming back to the community but the attacks that took place in 2001 and 2002 put the area in a state of high alert. During the early 1970's riots in Derry he'd crossed the barricades to treat Catholics who had been fired at by British troops using CS gas. He says that people in the Fountain are content to get on with a quiet life but at times feel at the mercy of Derry nationalists.

"When the attacks started two years ago people were very worried, it was the last thing we needed. Apart from posing a danger to the people already here it made our job of trying to convince people to move back much more difficult. At the very least the community's development would be held back by the attacks. We have been fighting a battle here to stay in existence for the past thirty years. When Bloody Sunday happened a lot of people moved out, they were afraid that they would be killed in revenge. Then when people got the chance to move out under redevelopment they never came back. It was only a few people who stayed here and for some of them it was because there was no choice but I would say that the Fountain has a good community spirit in it as well. We have come through the worst of the Troubles but really it wasn't until after 1985 that we felt very vulnerable. When the soldiers left the estate we felt as though there was nobody to protect us, a lot of people wished they had never left. Before that we were practically living in a military base and the odd mortar bomb coming over we could handle."

The social and economic history of Derry is bound up with the plantation and industrialisation of Ulster. Before the Troubles began Catholics and Protestants worked side by side in the city's many textile factories.

Although the factories are long gone Willie Temple believes the sectarianism in Derry is less acute than in Belfast, especially among the older generation.

"We don't have the same bitterness here that you would have in places like Belfast, there has always been a gentler feel to things here. For a start we aren't as big a place and because people worked together they still talk to each other on the streets. Despite the Troubles there has always been better community relations here than in other parts of the province. But the problem is with the teenagers, they are more liable to attack and they are harder to control."

Perhaps surprisingly, given the Fountain's geographical location in Derry, Willie Temple doesn't object to the idea of Derry being divided into two cities.

"It would give Unionists on the Waterside a better say in how things are run in that part of the town. With the numbers as they are on the Waterside Unionists would have a 50/50 split at a council over there. But it isn't going to happen because it would just be too impractical and the British Government wouldn't allow it. The town isn't big enough to warrant two councils really."

Derry city council was reconstituted in 1974 to redress the gerrymandering that had taken place since 1923. Since then it has had a nationalist majority with the SDLP the largest party and Sinn Féin coming a close second. The legacy of the Stormont era has had an impact on Derry's academic institutions.

The city's only University, Magee College, is seen as a poor cousin to the much larger University of Ulster Campus at Coleraine which was built in 1967. Many nationalists believe the university was built at Coleraine, a largely Protestant town some 40 miles away, because the Unionist government at Stormont didn't want a Catholic town to have its own University.

Nationalists and Unionists agree that although relations in Derry could be better they could also be much worse. Most politicians and community workers in Derry refer to each other in first name terms, and it is the only place in the North at the time of writing to have reached an accommodation on the marching issue.

In a break with protocol the Derry branch of the Apprentice Boys agreed to talk to the nationalist protesters at an early stage in the dispute. The move was controversial amongst the Loyal Orders with many accusing the local leadership of bowing to republican pressure. However, unlike their counterparts in

Dunloy and Bellaghy, the Apprentice Boys are able to march their full route around the city, unopposed every year. The basis of the deal was that the Apprentice Boys would be allowed to march but with conditions attached. At points of the route which touched nationalist areas bands would stop playing and the Apprentice Boys limited the number of people marching. But the particular condition which the Bogside residents attached to the deal was to get the Apprentice Boys to take responsibility for the thousands of supporters who came from all over the North to take part in the parade.

In the past bus-loads of loyalists travelling to Derry were involved in attacks on Catholic towns en route and many of these attacks were drink fuelled. Initially the Apprentice Boys resisted the condition but the sheer numerical superiority of Catholics in Derry put the residents in a strong position. Although some riots have broken out during the marches the two sides agree that it is a vast improvement on what went before.

Donnacha Mac Niallais is chairman of the Bogside Residents' Group which protested against the parades. He says it was difficult for nationalists to come to an accommodation but it was done in the best interests of the city.

"I don't like when people say that Derry should be held up as the model for all other areas of the North when it comes to resolving parades, because that is just putting too fine a gloss on it. It is renewed on a year by year basis and it is difficult at times. We can't always guarantee an agreement but at the same time we have worked, on both sides, to try and compromise. Derry is the birthplace of the Apprentice Boys so it has an importance to them, but they must understand the feelings of nationalists who make up the majority of the town. Without that respect there can be no deal. We were also concerned about other parades across the North such as the ones in the Lower Ormeau and the Garvaghy Road. That did factor into our thinking when we were talking to the Apprentice Boys."

Alistair Simpson, who lives in the Fountain Estate, was head of the Apprentice Boys when the deal was struck. He says that when he began talking to the residents the majority of Apprentice Boys were against it.

"I had to watch my back from people within my own constituency to be honest, I'd say 80% of members were against it and 20% for. Now that has reversed itself and there is a lot of support for it. We were talking to anyone who was interested, and we developed a strategy of putting ourselves forward as an historical organisation. The difference up here is that we are in a minority. Protestants in the west bank of Derry make up 1.5% of the population. If we don't get the agreement of the nationalist community things don't work. That's true from a business point of view as well. It was difficult talking to the Bogside residents group; they were trying to be dictatorial and tell us what to do and how to do it. The way we looked at it we were prepared to talk to anyone who was interested. We were able to do it in Derry because of the way the Apprentice Boys gives each branch autonomy to do things as they see fit. I explained it to members in an historical perspective. Our ancestors in the siege of Derry had to negotiate their way out, so that's what I told our members. Only time will tell if we were right. Getting walking in the city certainly gave people in the Fountain a boost. I still live in the estate and people were telling me that they felt better."

Alistair Simpson says people in the Fountain feel a sense of betrayal by other Unionists in Derry. He says Protestants in the Waterside aren't interested in what goes on in the Fountain.

"To be honest a lot of them don't give two stuffs about us over here. They don't want to know about us, because they are happy with how things are over there and why should they care about a few hundred of us. We have been let down badly in that way too. The main contact we have with the Waterside is through young people from here going over there for a drink, because they can't really drink in the West Bank."

Nowadays the Fountain has only one small grocers shop serving the community. Before the redevelopment in the 1970's Alistair Simpson says it was a much more vibrant community. Pam Mitchell is one of the oldest residents in the Fountain, she was one of the few who stayed through the redevelopment and two of her children choose to live there as well. Now in her late 70's she says she would never move out.

"I have always felt very close to the area. Despite all the trouble I've been blessed with good neighbours. I remember a time when the area was full of life and there were plenty of shops for everyone. It is much quieter now and there aren't too many original inhabitants left but there are still a few of us. I was worried sick when the attacks started up a while back, you worry for your kids and for yourself as well. I don't know how much longer the Fountain will be here but I hope I don't live to see the end of it."

Robin Percival is a sociology lecturer at Derry's North West Institute. An English-born Protestant he has carried out extensive research into the city's two principal interface communities, the Fountain and Gobnascale. He says that part of the problem with community development in the Fountain is due to the estate's growing reputation as a dumping ground for perceived problem families and an increasingly transient population.

"There are a number of divisions within the Fountain itself between people who have lived there for a longtime and the newer residents who are seen as "blowins". In 1972 the estate would have had a good sense of community to it, but today that doesn't exist. Some of the problems are to do with class, the high-levels of social deprivation and the frustration that breeds. Ritualised times of the year such as Celtic and Rangers matches and Apprentice Boys parades cause violence, especially now with the peace process. The big challenge from a sociological or political point of view would be to integrate the Fountain with the rest of Derry, but the reality is that a lot of people in the North want to live in segregated communities. When the two Protestant schools in the Fountain were integrated and became controlled schools there was great anxiety among residents because the history of controlled schools in Derry is one where they become overwhelmingly Catholic. But in some respects the Fountain enjoys benefits which other Protestant areas don't in terms of access to the commercial centre of Derry and in terms of access to places of worship for example."

Some of the sociological research carried out by Robin Percival and his colleagues appears to contradict the Unionist view that Protestants in the Fountain feel besieged and that the West Bank has no other Protestant communities.

He says that in research carried out in the mid-1990s by the Templegrove Action Unit, a cross-community research group of which he was chairman, Fountain residents didn't give sectarian threat as the major concern in the area. And he says that there is a significant minority of Protestants spread throughout Derry's nationalist population.

"In some ways it was fairly surprising, but the people there gave other issues as their concerns. Although Protestants talk about the exodus from Derry that doesn't actually stand up to scrutiny. While its true that their numbers have reduced dramatically in the Fountain that isn't entirely down to sectarian factors. It is interesting that in Limavady, a traditionally Protestant town, there is now a Catholic majority yet Unionist politicians don't talk of an exodus from Limavady. In many ways economic factors, principally house prices, have driven population change in places like Derry. That can't be separated from political changes but the reality is that for first-time buyers a house in a Protestant area is usually significantly cheaper than its equivalent in a Catholic area."

Mitchell McLaughlin is Sinn Féin's national chairman and an MLA for Derry. He has lived in the city all his life and says that nationalists and republicans have tried to extend the hand of friendship to Unionists. He says there have been genuine attempts to reach out, but at times those attempts have been misunderstood, sometimes because of a fear within Unionism.

"We see it as a particular challenge and a necessary task to demonstrate that we can respect the rights, cultures and traditions of others. In that respect there are very genuine efforts to reach out. It doesn't mean that people always understand it. The Unionist reaction is sometimes based on paranoia rather than the reaction of a confident community. That feeling is reinforced by people like Gregory [Campbell] who is more interested in making statements for party political reasons rather than as a helpful way to sort out

problems. That means it can take longer to get dialogue up and running than it sometimes should, but it
is well worth the effort."

While critical of Gregory Campbell's approach to
community relations in Derry, McLaughlin says community workers such as Willie Temple and politicians
such as the DUP's Willie Hay have provided leadership
for their community.

"There are a lot of people on the Unionist side who
want to see better community relations established
and will show leadership in doing that. People like Willie
Hay were very good at facilitating dialogue between
the Apprentice Boys and Bogside residents. He mightn't
like to be praised by a Sinn Féin member but it is the
truth. When the DUP as a party start engaging with Sinn
Féin, which they will do, it will make solving the problem a lot easier. They will do it eventually but it is just a
question of when."

In terms of Protestant feelings of exclusion from the
town Mitchell McLaughlin believes that Unionists have
imposed a virtual economic boycott on Derry because
most businesses in the town are Catholic owned.

He argues that pre-1969 Protestants were happy to
shop in the town because the town's commerce was
controlled by fellow Protestants.

"There has been a drift away from Derry by some
Protestants. They have moved down the coast to
places like Coleraine and Limavady. A lot of them no
longer shop in Derry but I think a part of that is down to

a sectarian attitude among some. They are less comfortable giving money to Catholic shop owners than to Protestant ones, which I think is quite a sectarian attitude really. Sectarianism was never as bad in Derry as it is some parts of Belfast for example. I think Protestants should ask themselves why it is that in a city with a majority nationalist community the sectarianism hasn't been as bad. But really what needs to happen is that dialogue needs to continue, eventually the efforts will be reciprocated and it is very important for nationalists and republicans in Derry to demonstrate that there is a way forward."

Loyalist critics challenge the rosy picture portrayed by Sinn Féin. Outsiders in particular point out what they see as the distinct Catholic/republican ethos of the city-side. That this perception is widespread is demonstrated by the reluctance of Protestant businessmen to invest there, with many having fresh memories of the IRA bombing campaign against Protestant and British owned businesses. Fears (real and imagined) of a renewal of another such campaign is a real obstacle to investment. Fear of crime is also a deterrent for potential Protestant businessmen in an area where the PSNI is not universally accepted.

However, Mitchell McLaughlin points to the fact that nationalists in Derry took attacks on the Fountain seriously enough to hold a public meeting about them.

"The message was spelt out very clearly that sectarian attacks on the Fountain were not acceptable, indeed no sort of attack whatsoever. I, as a Sinn Féin member told those involved to stop it, that isn't what we are about and there can be no place for that in our society. Adults actually volunteered to go down to the interface and make sure that the teenagers were kept away, and that happened. I know even people in the Fountain would agree that we played a constructive role in bring that spurt of attacks to an end."

However past efforts by Sinn Féin to show the hand of friendship haven't been met with such a favourable response. In the late 1980's Sinn Féin councillors, along with Unionists, voted for a funding package for a commemoration of Lundy's day, one of the most important historical events in the calendar for Protestants. Lundy was a Protestant traitor hanged for his part in trying to help the Catholic besiegers of Derry's Protestants in the 1600's. As part of the proposal Sinn Féin delegated one of their members to write an opening speech retelling the history of the day. The speech was to be read at a special play put on for schoolchildren in the city, but when the day arrived most Protestant schools had boycotted the event because of Sinn Féin involvement.

· · · · · · · ·

Gobnascale is in some ways the mirror image of the Fountain. It is a nationalist enclave in a mainly Unionist part of the Waterside.

But there are no security walls built around it and the 2,500 people who live there are confident of the future. Over the years there have been sectarian clashes at the interface with Robin Street. The area has been targeted by loyalist paramilitaries, the worst incident was in December 1972 when five people were killed in a loyalist gun attack on Annie's Bar. At the start of 2003 there was talk of putting up a CCTV camera system, similar to those at interfaces in Belfast, but nationalists were against the plan. Tensions at Gobnascale are at their worst during the Apprentice Boys marches in Derry. For most of the morning and afternoon the area is sealed off by police and army and residents complain they can't get to the town centre.

Trouble is sometimes sparked off by the influx of loyalists to the town for the Orange Order marches. Most young people from Gobnascale socialise in the West Bank and have to arrange taxis home because of the threat of sectarian attacks. Although Protestants point to the demise of their community in Derry's West Bank the same could also have been said for the Catholic community in the Waterside which hadn't grown for almost 20 years according to the 1991 census. This trend has been reversed in the 2001 census however.

The figures suggested that Catholics were choosing to move way from the Waterside and onto the West Bank, despite higher house prices. Although community workers in Gobnascale say more Catholics are choosing to live in the Waterside since 1994, partly due to peace and partly because of cheaper house prices.

Ciaran O'Donnell is a community worker in Gobnascale. His uncle, Bernard Kelly, was one of the five people killed in the Annie's bar attack. He says that although the threat of interface violence is always present the realities of high unemployment levels and social deprivation are just as big a problem for the community.

"Catholics here don't feel as threatened as they would do in other interface areas because, at the end of the day, we are in a majority in the city as a whole but that doesn't mean we don't feel threatened. There have been sectarian attacks on people here and it is a constant danger especially at the edges of the estate which border on to the Protestant streets. We have relatively good contact with Protestant community workers and we try to meet them regularly enough. But there is always the unwritten rule that you don't talk about political issues so most of the time is spent talking about things which are fairly non-contentious, although at least there is a line of communication there. We suffer badly from economic deprivation in the area, around 60% of the adult male population is long-term unemployed or on some sort of benefit. We don't have proper resources for the community so teenagers who are going off the rails a bit don't have a safety net to fall back on. All of those things make the problems of interfaces worse, because those factors can lead to trouble in themselves. We also have a bad relationship with the cops, like most nationalist areas. But the cops seem to harbour a particular grudge against Gobnascale. They seem keen to present the area in the worst possible way and that's one reason why we are opposed to these security cameras going up. We think there has been a concerted effort by the PSNI to portray the area in a bad light just to have these cameras put up."

• • • • • • • •

We often hear in the news bulletins relating to the Middle East the mention of a "two state solution", i.e., a separate Palestinian state existing beside Israel. Well, what comes across from some of the unionist contributors to this chapter is their desire for a "two city solution", i.e., a protestant Londonderry on the Waterside (east of the River Foyle) and a catholic Derry on the West Bank (another Middle East connotation).

It would be hard to argue that such segregation would address the issues of tolerance of different traditions, unless such separateness would create a "respite" from any siege mentality. Of course the traditions are not just "different" but, diametrically opposed in political, national and religious terms. It is this challenge that is being addressed by those on the ground.

Chapter 6
Lower Ormeau, Belfast

The interface area in Belfast most identified with protests against Loyal Order parades is the Lower Ormeau in the south of the city. It was here in 1992 that nationalist residents of the area first staged street protests against the annual Apprentice Boys Parade which marched down the Ormeau Road every Easter Monday and Twelfth of July.

Since then the district has witnessed demonstrations and counter-demonstrations by residents and the Loyal Orders, each equally determined that their demands be met. But for the first time Lower Ormeau spokesman Gerard Rice, reveals here that if the Apprentice Boys had agreed to cancel their Easter Parade in 1992 residents would probably have dropped plans for further protests. However, along with the Garvaghy Road in Portadown, it became one of the focal points for the highly contentious marching season.

As the British Government, local politicians and the

Parades Commission scrambled around to find a resolution to the marching season the Lower Ormeau was regarded as one of the most important for finding an accommodation to suit all sides. Politicians thought that if a solution to the dispute could be found in the Lower Ormeau it could be found anywhere.

Although nationalists had always resented the parades, which they regard as triumphalist and sectarian, there was very little organised protest against them. Nationalists in the Lower Ormeau resent being cordoned into the area for most of the day to facilitate the parade and insist that in order to march the Loyal Orders should engage in dialogue with the community. The Apprentice Boys and Orange Order say marching down the Lower Ormeau is part of their traditional route and claim they have compromised by reducing the number of bands and stopping playing music as they pass nationalist houses.

The Lower Ormeau is a compact community made up of a network of narrow streets stretching on one side from Cromac Square to the Ormeau Bridge and backing onto the River Lagan. It has a total population of just over 2,500 people and until the mid-1960's was predominantly Protestant and working-class. Most Protestants left the area before the onset of the Troubles for better houses in the then newly built Belvoir Estate in South Belfast; nationalists gladly bought up the newly vacated houses and by the early 1970's the area was predominantly Catholic.

Although the Upper Ormeau has a significant nationalist community, it has always been middle-class and trouble free, the Catholics who live there are surrounded by Protestant estates. The Lower Ormeau also faces onto the staunchly loyalist Donegall Pass area of South Belfast. A small peace line was erected there in the mid-1990s to stop stone-throwing incidents but the junction with the Lower Ormeau has continued to be the scene of some vicious riots.

For years the Apprentice Boys had paraded past the Lower Ormeau, and despite the changing demographics continued to do so throughout the Troubles. Often the bands who took part were little more than what is colloquially known as 'Kick the Pope Bands' - blood and thunder loyalists drumming out sectarian tunes.

The one event that exacerbated the residents' protests was the Ormeau Road Betting shop massacre of February 1992. On a Wednesday morning on 17 February 1992 a UFF gang walked into Sean Graham's Betting shop on the Ormeau Road and sprayed it with automatic gunfire. Five Catholics were shot dead and dozens injured, all of the dead coming from the Lower Ormeau.

The murders horrified and angered the Lower Ormeau community and by the summer of 1992 the first scenes of nationalists protesting for Apprentice Boys and Orange Order parades to be rerouted appeared on television. Four weeks later a residents committee from the Lower Ormeau demanded the parade be rerouted away from the area to prevent trouble and as a mark of respect to the dead. However the Apprentice Boys refused to reroute.

Nationalist anger at the decision was made even worse when some of the people following the march gave a five-fingered salute outside the betting shop. Nationalists also accused the Apprentice Boys of deliberately beating their drums louder outside the shop, adding insult to injury. One of the five-fingered culprits was later severely disciplined by the Loyal Order.

Gerard Rice, is a community worker in the Lower Ormeau and was one of the key figures involved in the dispute. He has lived in the area since the 1960's. He says that if the Apprentice Boys had agreed to reroute in 1992 it is likely the protest would have been a one-off.

"People were naturally hurt, fearful and angered by the betting shop massacre. We decided that as a mark of respect to the victims the Apprentice Boys should reroute away from the Lower Ormeau that Easter Monday to let the community grieve in peace. First of all we went through the courts and the issue became public in that way but we had no success and the Apprentice Boys simply refused to even consider rerouting away from the area. When they did come down that year their numbers had swelled from the usual 200 or so to around 5,000 and people from the area simply couldn't believe they were so intent on causing grief and sectarianism. The bands even stopped outside the house of a woman whose son had been shot dead by loyalists in 1987 and beat their drums louder. People here were incensed and the behaviour of the RUC just compounded that. They beat us off the street and cordoned off the area to allow a sectarian parade. But what really hardened attitudes here was when one of the people following the Apprentice Boys Parade gave a five fingered salute outside the betting shop where the five people were killed. We knew exactly what that meant and were determined to make sure the parades would be stopped from marching through our area, especially when the people organising them refused to even speak to us or ask us for our consent."

Catholics in the Lower Ormeau have suffered disproportionately at the hands of loyalist terrorists. An estimated 30 people from the area have been killed by the UDA and UVF over the course of the Troubles. Because of the area's proximity to loyalist areas such as Donegall Pass and Annadale it has been an easy target for loyalist terrorists. Gunmen would sometimes drive into the area and shoot-up houses before speeding off.

One such attack claimed the life of Theresa Clinton a 33 year-old mother of two. She was killed when UDA gunmen fired bullets through her living room window on April 14 1994. The localised nature of the violence was illustrated when four months later the IRA killed two leading loyalists suspected of taking part in the murder. The pair were killed less than a mile away from Theresa Clinton's home, while the IRA men who carried out the shooting escaped into the Lower Ormeau.

When a police patrol pursued the gunmen into one of the streets, they were attacked by a crowd and had to retreat. The police would comment that such incidents would not be untypical and would further point out that many attacks on the security forces originated from the Lower Ormeau.

Despite the protests all the parades were given the go-ahead up until 1995, the first marching season after the IRA and UVF/UDA ceasefires of 1994. Ironically the last time a parade was approved was in Easter 2001, but the Foot and Mouth crisis forced organisers to cancel.

In 1998 the Orange Order marched down the Lower Ormeau the day after three Catholic children were murdered in Ballymoney by loyalists calling for all Orange Marches to go ahead. The Lower Ormeau Residents dubbed the parade a march of shame and stood silently by the roadside holding black flags in memory of the children. They also released black balloons before the march began. Although the Orange Order refrained from playing music as it walked by the Lower Ormeau, many felt it was a moral victory for the residents and since then the Orange Order hasn't marched on the road.

A number of other incidents during Orange marches in the Lower Ormeau had served to deepen resentment among nationalists. Not least of which was an event in 1992 when a Protestant woman following the Apprentice Boys parade danced outside the Lower Ormeau betting shop.

After 1995 the anti-marching protests became more widespread and in a new strategy the Lower Ormeau community called on nationalists from across the North to come to the area and support them.

The call had the effect of widening the protest and providing the Lower Ormeau community with extra numbers for the demonstrations. For their part the Apprentice Boys gathered at the bridge which separates the traditionally Protestant Upper Ormeau from the Lower Ormeau. Every banned parade met with apocalyptic threats to bring Unionists and loyalists onto the streets of Northern Ireland. Protestants from across the North rallied behind them and loyalists blocked off roads in Belfast and other towns.

Occasionally riots with the RUC and British Army broke out, and just like nationalists in the Lower Ormeau, the Apprentice Boys and Orange Order found common cause with their counterparts in the Garvaghy Road, Bellaghy and Dunloy. As Drumcree enraged unionists and loyalists, so too did the sight of Orangemen and the RUC anger nationalists. As the dispute dragged on through the uncertain years of the peace process it became clear to all that a resolution in the Lower Ormeau would affect protests in other flashpoints across Northern Ireland

Both residents and marchers accused the British Government of engaging in political trade-offs and appeasement by banning one contentious parade while allowing another to go-ahead. When Mo Mowlam became secretary of state for Northern Ireland in 1997 she visited the Lower Ormeau residents and the Apprentice Boys, such was the importance attached to the area's problems.

The main spokesman for the Apprentice Boys during the height of the protests was Noel Liggett. A former baker, he became the face of Apprentice Boys anger and dismay at the Parades dispute. For the first six years of the dispute he refused to talk to the Lower Ormeau residents because their chief spokesman, Gerard Rice, had a conviction for firearms offences. He says that even today the widely-held perception in the Unionist community is that all the protests were organised and manipulated by Sinn Féin to gain votes.

"We simply wanted to walk down the road without causing offence to anyone. We weren't there to offend nationalists, we were and still are taking part in a peaceful march that has been taking place for generations, and we have been walking the route since 1887. It is clear that there are people in the Lower Ormeau who are organising the protests for their own benefit; there were republican hands at work. They were interested in making political gain out of the situation as opposed to anything else, and we weren't going to allow them to get that. Unlike the Catholic community we didn't recognise the differences, we regard the community as one. At the end of the day we live on the Ormeau Road as well, we travel up and down it every day to work and to the town".

Although talks between the two sides did take place in the late 90's very little came out of them and at present there is no face-to-face dialogue. Whereas nationalists link the death of the three Quinn children to the parades dispute, unionists emphatically deny the claim. And they say that allegations of bands gloating over sectarian deaths refer to isolated incidents.

Noel Liggett argues the importance of marching for the Protestant community has been totally overlooked by nationalists.

"The parades help to unite what is a very diverse Protestant community in Northern Ireland, that is why we attach such significance to them. Nationalists are intent on deriding them at every opportunity. I accept that the five fingers being held up outside the Ormeau Road betting shop was a disgraceful gesture but that is something outside of our control."

It has to be said that there are more than 3,000 Loyal Order marches across the North every year, with only a handful of them being contested by nationalists. When nationalist protests became vocal and organised the organisation which had the final ruling on the parade was the RUC. This led to inevitable difficulties since nationalists accused the RUC, which was 93% Protestant, of being biased in favour of Orange marches. As a result the Parades Commission was established by the British Government in 1997 to make rulings on whether or not a parade could go ahead. The idea was that a body judged to be nonpartisan could gain the trust of both communities and any rulings would be better accepted.

However at various times both nationalists and unionists have lambasted it, depending on the decision it has made. Noel Liggett says it has added to the problems in the Lower Ormeau.

"People have no faith in the body whatsoever. It has been all over the place since it first began and it has not treated Protestants fairly at all. We would see it as being biased in favour of nationalists and it has created more problems than anything else."

More often than not protests against the marches ended in riots on the Lower Ormeau. Residents accused the RUC of heavy-handedness and pointed to the fact that they were cordoned into their area for almost an entire day because the Apprentice Boys return parade did not make its way up the Ormeau Road until seven in the evening. Lines of RUC Land Rovers blocked off the streets that make-up the Lower Ormeau while the parade passed by. In effect residents were hemmed into their own area for hours on end. In one instance a gunman appeared from a street opposite the Hatfield Bar and fired shots at the RUC in broad daylight. However the isolated geography of the Lower Ormeau meant that it could be easily contained. The RUC said that it was acting to ensure the safety of both residents and marchers.

Sinn Féin's Alex Maskey, an MLA for South Belfast and the city's first republican Lord Mayor, says people were incensed by the RUC's behaviour.

"They were really doing the Orangemen's work for them - they were blocking people into the area to facilitate the parade. They were lined out in full riot gear, plastic bullets guns at the ready and it was very intimidating for the residents. This was their area after all and there were kids and grandparents being blocked in to their own homes. It is also worth remembering that most people in the Lower Ormeau regard the RUC as the armed wing of unionism and would have been aware of their collusion with the UDA and UFF. The guns used to kill the five people in the betting shop were shipped to loyalists by the British Military Intelligence Services." alleges Maskey.

At one stage the Lower Ormeau became the focal point for anti-marching protests in Belfast. The Reverend Martin Smyth is the UUP MP for South Belfast and until 1995 was leader of the Orange Lodge in Ireland. A lifelong Orangeman, he was Grand Master of the Order from 1972 until 1995, he was opposed to talks with residents groups. During the marching dispute he refused to meet with the Lower Ormeau residents, who were his constituents, but gave permission to his deputy, Robert Saulters, to negotiate. Smyth's refusal to talk to the Lower Ormeau residents and his participation in the marches was widely condemned by nationalist politicians and human rights groups. He says that incidents such as the five-fingered salute and the woman dancing outside the betting shop have been misconstrued.

And he insists that marching down the Lower Ormeau the day after the Quinn children's deaths was right.

"I held out the hand of friendship to the Lower Ormeau community at a rally we had to commemorate the Anniversary of the Anglo-Irish agreement, but it was rejected out of hand. I never met with the residents group because I didn't see it as a bona fide group, it was more of a front for Sinn Féin. The five-fingered salute was a simple misunderstanding, the man was being jeered at by republicans and he was just telling them to go away. My wife was there and she told me that. As for the woman dancing it was foolish but I don't think any particular disrespect was made. People criticised us for marching down after the Quinn deaths but we weren't responsible and we did agree to march down without music. Someone even suggested that we should lay a wreath but I thought that might be misinterpreted by the protesters so we decided not to. The first year the protest began I was head of the Order and I gave my permission for Robert Saulters to talk with them. He came away with an agreement that wasn't adhered to."

The agreement made between the residents and Robert Saulters contained four main points. The Orange Order would be allowed to march down the

Ormeau Road on July 12, the Royal Black Preceptory would be allowed to march in August and crucially that any future parades would only go ahead if the Lower Ormeau community gave their consent at a public meeting. The two sides also agreed to work together to improve community relations in the area.

The deal was struck on the eve of the Drumcree march and as it was about to be announced on radio the RUC forced the Orangemen through the Garvaghy Road. Robert Saulters read only the first two points on radio and said the third point couldn't be agreed to as he couldn't guarantee he'd be in the Orange Order the following year. Debate still surrounds the deal but Gerard Rice says it was made clear that if the Orange Order didn't accept it there would be protests at every parade on the Lower Ormeau. He says nationalists were willing to compromise and didn't rule out future parades but the Orange Order were loathe to accept the principal of consent.

"They didn't want to accept that they would have to get the agreement of the community if they wanted to march down. It seemed sort of pointless in talking to them at times, but we still wanted to do it. What we had every year was the Orange Order refusing to talk to us at all but still insisting on marching through our community. They came up with a hundred reasons not to talk, but the bottom line was that they don't want to negotiate a way through because they see themselves as superior to the residents. They were only encouraged in that by the RUC who were more than willing to push them down the road."

The 1995 meeting was the last ever held between the two sides.

Aside from the marching dispute the Lower Ormeau lies just opposite from the loyalist stronghold of Donegall Pass and a number of Catholics have been shot dead at the point where the Donegall Pass meets the Lower Ormeau Road. More recently the area has witnessed sectarian clashes and some Protestant residents demanded an extra security fence which was added at the point where the two areas back on to each other.

All was not totally bleak in the area as a number of years after the abortive meeting in 1995 a mobile phone network was established by community workers on both sides. The system allows community workers to nip trouble in the bud, although it does have to be said that it doesn't always work.

Catholic and Protestant houses at the interface have both had specially designed with laminated glass fitted to guard against stone-throwers. However, despite the trouble which took place across Belfast in the summer of 2002 the area remained relatively quiet, with only some minor incidents. When violence did occur in the Donegall Pass in the summer of 2002 it was chiefly between loyalists and the police. The rioting last for three days and cars and restaurants were burned out by petrol bombers.

Although both communities are solidly working-class

they are just yards from Belfast's Golden Mile area, a hub for the city's student and tourist population. The Donegall Pass violence was condemned by senior Unionist politicians who said it discouraged tourism. Dawn Purvis is a PUP member based in Donegall Pass, an area with a high proportion of elderly people. She says there is no appetite for violence amongst the residents.

"When there was trouble people became sick of it very quickly; they realised they were the ones who had to live with it every night. People don't want that sort of trouble. It is usually started by people who don't have to live in the houses that get attacked later that night. The last time there would have been significant trouble was when the Celtic and Rangers games were on. You get people drunk coming out of pubs and the next thing is there is rioting in the street, but that has been about it."

Since the late 1990's Celtic and Rangers matches have become excuses for trouble at interfaces across Northern Ireland. The trouble after them became so ritualised that in 2002 the PSNI asked a court to order the Cave Hill Inn, a predominantly Protestant bar in north Belfast, to close during a game. Most observers agree that during the Troubles there wasn't as much trouble associated with the games. Dawn Purvis says that interface violence in other parts of Belfast puts a strain on community relations.

"We had to try a lot harder to make sure trouble didn't start in this part of town when the violence was all over the place. It took real effort when the Short Strand went bad but we were able to contain it all. We did it through the mobile phone network. It doesn't always work but it is better than nothing."

Although the mobile phone network exists the two communities are polarised mentally and physically isolated from each other. There are, for example, two post offices, each used almost exclusively by only one community.

When Protestants in the Donegall Pass called for a security fence at the back of houses facing onto the Lower Ormeau to stop trouble, nationalists accused them of engineering the violence. Gerard Rice says the common perception in the Lower Ormeau was that Protestants wanted to use the violence as an excuse to further secure the area against outsiders.

"They called for the security fence after the trouble began but it wasn't people on our side causing the trouble. Although there is no peace line around Donegall Pass there is a normal wall the whole way round it. I would look at the area and see somewhere with a siege mentality. They react very aggressively sometimes and the idea for a security wall was only scrapped when some of the Protestant residents said they didn't want it either. All of a sudden the trouble stopped."

• • • • • • • •

Whether it has been the mobile telephone network or other factors the Lower Ormeau has been relatively peaceful since 1998 with community workers on both sides able to work together reasonably well at times. Perhaps one of the factors in this stability is that the Lower Ormeau has a more settled community and therefore a better infrastructure. However, one adverse economic effect of the area's reputation has been the virtual disappearance of Protestant-owned businesses, due to fear and perceived intimidation.

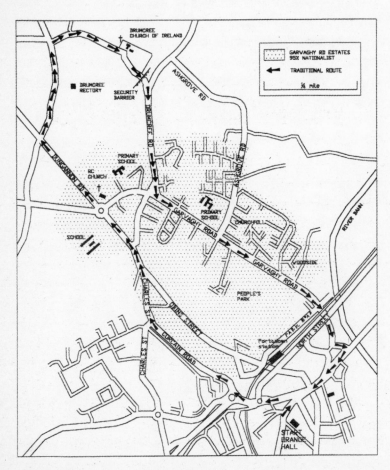

In recent years a symbolic letter of protest was delivered at the security barrier. The return march then took place along the earlier route via Dungannon Road.

Chapter 7

Drumcree and the Garvaghy Road

In 1995 the quiet parish of Drumcree on the outskirts of the mainly loyalist town of Portadown in County Armagh, made worldwide news. Vivid televised scenes of marching Orangemen with their bands, ugly street rioting with petrol bombs were broadcast around the world. Drumcree – the name itself destined to mark another emotive chapter in the history of The Troubles – was in the spotlight.

It became synonymous with Parades Disputes that eight years later still damaged relations between Unionists and nationalists.

For it was here that the Orange Order faced a ban from marching down the Garvaghy Road for the first time in its history. The decision, made by the RUC on security grounds, sparked rage amongst Orangemen who regard Portadown as the birthplace of the Order. Orange leaders and Unionist politicians united to demand the right to march down the mainly nationalist

Garvaghy Road on the last Sunday before the Twelfth of July, a commemoration of the thousands of Ulstermen who died at the Somme in World War I.

Unionists and loyalists of all shades gathered in the field beside Drumcree Church in their tens of thousands and threatened to remain there until the decision was reversed. They claimed that banning them from marching was tantamount to denying them their civil and religious liberties. In the event the decision was reversed and the Orange Order was forced through the Garvaghy Road against the wishes of the residents. The Garvaghy Road residents said the march was an infringement of their human rights. They argued that an alternative route along the Corcraine Road was available which would cause offence to no-one. They, like most Catholics, regard the parade as triumphalist, and said Orangemen had no right to march through their part of the town without first trying to gain their consent.

After the six minute parade had passed, many local Garvaghy Road residents and supporters engaged in running battles with the RUC.

As the protest amongst Orangemen grew hard-line loyalist gunmen such as Billy Wright, leader of the anti-ceasefire LVF and which was then engaged in a campaign to kill Catholics, was seen mingling in the large crowd, that also included Unionist leaders such as Ian Paisley and David Trimble, in the grounds of Drumcree church overlooking the Garvaghy Road. It is a matter of some regret that the author was unable to obtain a contribution from the local MP, Mr Trimble, one of the few people who refused to talk to the author in his research for this book.

Not since the days of the Anglo-Irish agreement and subsequent protests had unionism came together in such numbers with one common aim. For days it seemed to many as if Northern Ireland was teetering on the brink of civil war as many on the Unionists side appeared to threaten to bring the state to its knees if their brethren were not allowed to march the traditional route down the Garvaghy Road. In what became known as 'Drumcree I' a cycle of protest and counter-protest began which still affects Northern Ireland today.

Since 1998, the Orange Order has been banned by the Parades Commission from marching along the Garvaghy Road but thousands of Protesters still turned up to confront the British Army and police, and to demand the right to march. Many Unionists feel that this decision was a sop to Nationalism, brought about by threats of disorder and violent protest. However, nationalist would suggest that in the years 1995-1997 the RUC escorted the Orange Order down the road, fearing that to ban the march would spark violent protests by loyalist. Bríd Rogers of the moderate SDLP has referred to this period as marking "the end of the RUC in Catholic areas."

The march is one of around 40 that takes place in

Portadown every year but is the only one which nationalists actively oppose. In past years the Orange Order marched through the other nationalist enclave of Portadown, Obin Street. The marches were usually marked by riots and eventually the Obin Street district was sealed off from the rest of the town by a huge security wall.

The Obin Street residents succeeded in having the Orange March rerouted away from their area in 1985 and 1986. Loyalists showed their anger by turning on the Garvaghy Road in 1986. In the early hours of the morning a mob of around 400 people smashed windows and cars in the Garvaghy Road area reinforcing a feeling of isolation within the nationalist community in Portadown.

The Obins Street events were a virtual reverse of an earlier clash on 17th March 1985. St Patrick's Accordion Band had received from the RUC permission to parade from Obins Street, along Garvaghy Road and Park Road, en route to a bus, which would take them to a major St Patrick's Day celebration at Cookstown. Park Road is a mainly Protestant area. Enraged Loyalists organised a protest, which took the form of a religious service on the footpaths of the Park Road route. For the duration of the band and its supporters' parade, a large crowd had assembled for the protest. Local Protestant residents expressed concern at the possible confrontation and demanded police protection against possible attack. Although the RUC were out in strength, the parade approval was rescinded to prevent a serious breach of the peace. The Protestant protesters had stopped the parade.

In the evening, the return parade was also banned by the RUC (this was 11 years before the Parades Commission took responsibility for such decisions). Loyalists claim that in response, nationalists attacked Protestant homes in the Woodside area beside Garvaghy Road. Nationalist politicians claimed that the police should have protected the parade and allowed it through despite the protests. The RUC was accused of giving in to threats of violence, perhaps a logical conclusion for a frustrated community to reach. However, the same conclusion was reached by Protestants when their marches on Garvaghy Road were banned years later due to what they saw as threats of violence by Catholic residents. It might appear to a neutral observer faintly ironic that the views on marching often change depending on who is doing the marching.

Breandán Mac Cionnaith, who went to prison for an attack on the Portadown British Legion Hall many years ago, was chairman of the Garvaghy Road residents. Originally from Obin Street he says nationalists have always felt vulnerable in Portadown. He says loyalists in the town have always wanted to ghettoise the Catholic community.

"The Orange Marches are about reinforcing that ghettoisation. It is about telling Catholics in the town that they are second-class citizens and that the loyalists rule the place. I lived in Obin Street throughout the Troubles and we were always under attack from loyalists. It was always understood that if you were a Catholic you were a target and that Obin Street was a general target because that's where all the Catholics lived. Then every year you had Orange Order parades marching down the street and everyone had to stay in their houses for the day. The same people marching down banging drums shouting 'kill all Taigs' were the same people who were trying to kill you the rest of the year. There is a very basic indignity in that which is clear for everyone to see. Catholics in Obin Street started to move out because of the nonstop attacks which is why the eight estates around the Garvaghy Road are now the main nationalist part of the town. Catholics sought refuge in numbers and when we opposed the Orangemen marching through our streets we were beaten off the road by the RUC. It has to be remembered many of the people who now live in the Garvaghy Road moved there because loyalists had intimidated them out of their homes in other parts of the town. Catholics certainly feel very marginalized in Portadown. It isn't safe for us to walk into town and the fact that the NIO built a huge wall around us is proof of the intimidation we suffered."

One day in July 1985 Orangemen marched up and down Obin Street four times. Bríd Rogers is deputy leader of the SDLP and based in Portadown. A former Agriculture Minister in the Stormont Executive, she says the night ended with masked gunmen searching people's houses.

"The RUC had escorted them up and down and people in Obin Street were very angry and intimidated by the parades. Later that night masked gunmen actually went into Catholic houses at the edge of Obin Street searching out victims. They destroyed houses as well. The residents there had been protesting about the Orange Parades for a few years but that night brought things to a head."

After the incident, the then RUC Chief Constable Jack Hermon, visited Obin Street under armed guard, and declared that from then on Orange Order parades wouldn't be allowed to parade there. But controversially he ruled that the Garvaghy Road was suitable because it was an arterial route and not a nationalist area.

One important factor in the level of protest on the Garvaghy Road is the population shift which has been continuing over a number of years. Today the whole Obin Street area is home to around 500 people, many of its residents having moved to the Garvaghy Road during the 1970's and 80's. The two areas sit side by side in the town's northwestern corner. Catholics make up about a quarter of Portadown's 28,000 population.

Garvaghy Road was not originally 100% Catholic. One of the estates in the area, the Churchill estate, was a mixed estate. However, as the Troubles escalated, and particularly during the time of the Hunger strikes, many Protestants were intimidated out of that estate.

As stated earlier the town has a special place in the history of Protestant culture in the Northern Ireland as it is the birthplace of the Orange Order. During the early years of the protest widespread loyalist violence took place across the North. During the period of the Drumcree march virtually every main road was blocked, often by small numbers of men, sometimes by teenagers and women and for days all movement was stopped. The RUC said they were loathe to move in on protests for fear of inflaming passions which they said were already high. By the time the protest fizzled out in 2000, 12 people had been killed as a direct result of them. Catholics in Portadown felt particularly vulnerable.

For many years during the trouble Portadown was one of the most active areas for loyalist paramilitaries. At least a dozen Catholics were killed in the town centre alone, with some of the most high-profile murders taking place in the late 1990's.

The solicitor for the Garvaghy Road residents, Rosemary Nelson, was murdered by a loyalist car bomb in 1999 and her death became the focus for demands for a public inquiry into state collusion with loyalist paramilitaries. As in many other interface areas the marching dispute on the Garvaghy Road polarised an already deeply divided community. Catholics claimed that they couldn't use the town centre, except in emergencies, after a Catholic man, Robert Hamill, was kicked to death by a crowd of loyalists. It emerged later that a police patrol parked across the street had witnessed the attack but failed to intervene.

During the standoffs the Orange Order refused to talk to the residents. Eventually in 1997 what became known as proximity talks between the Garvaghy residents and the Orange Order were organised. Each side sat in separate rooms and talked to each other through intermediaries. In the highly-charged atmosphere of Drumcree a compromise wasn't reached.

Later that summer loyalist paramilitaries threatened to kill anyone providing services to the Garvaghy Road. By this stage the dispute had taken on a life of its own and Drumcree had become the focus of Northern Ireland's political tensions.

When in 1995, 1996 and 1997 the RUC baton-charged Garvaghy Road residents and supporters staging a sit-down protest off the road to force the Orange Parade through, nationalists compared it to their treatment during the Civil Rights marches in 1969. They also accused the British Government of buckling to Unionist threats of violence. On each occasion, parts of Northern Ireland had been brought to a virtual standstill by loyalists supporting Drumcree. In 1996, the road leading to the Larne ferry terminal, connecting Northern Ireland to Scotland, was blocked off by loyalists. For many nationalists, these events convinced them that nothing had really changed in thirty years.

The parade's importance to Unionism was highlighted when both Ian Paisley and David Trimble visited 10 Downing Street in the days before the march to tell John Major they would withdraw support for him in the House of Commons if it wasn't allowed to go ahead. Since 1998, however, the Orange Order has been banned by the Parades Commission from walking down the Garvaghy Road, leading to further clashes between Loyalists and the security forces. The British Army was forced to erect a 'mobile' peace line at the Garvaghy Road to stop loyalists from gaining access to the Garvaghy Road area, and during the height of the dispute an extra 2,000 British troops were drafted into Northern Ireland to help deal with the trouble caused.

Nationalists were critical of the RUC's handling of the Drumcree dispute. Bríd Rogers says that during the four-day stand off in 1996, which ended when the RUC forced the parade through, masked loyalists had been allowed to seal off roads around Portadown.

"That day was the most horrendous experience of my political life. For four days the community was under siege and it only ended when the RUC beat people off the road. They had allowed loyalists to take control of Portadown and on that day I think it was the end for the RUC in nationalist areas. People witnessed the scenes all over the North and realised that the RUC had acted in a very unfair way. At that time it summed up the Northern Ireland state and Catholics place in it."

Portadown and its surrounding areas has become a stronghold for loyalist paramilitaries throughout the Troubles. Its strong links to loyalist terrorism were shown in 1998 when the town came to a standstill for the funeral of Billy Wright, a self-confessed sectarian killer. Businesses and shops in the town closed for the day, some under threat of violence, to show a mark of respect for Billy Wright, who had been murdered by INLA inmates of the Maze prison.

Portadown was also the focal point for loyalist dissent against the peace process. It was here that Billy Wright set up the Loyalist Volunteer Force, a splinter group from the larger UVF. Its aim was to keep killing Catholics in spite of the peace process.

In July 1996 they murdered Catholic taxi driver Michael McGoldrick. The man who pulled the trigger later admitting he had killed McGoldrick as a birthday present for Billy Wright. At the time the LVF said it killed him because the Orange Order was being prevented from marching the Garvaghy Road. It also emerged that the terror group had planned to kidnap a group of Catholic priests and kill them one by one if the march was not allowed to go ahead. Breandán Mac Cionnaith says that the murders were aimed at stopping the anti-marching protests.

"It was clear what they were at, but we had no choice on the Garvaghy Road. Our demand was reasonable, we wanted them to talk to us and come to a compromise but they were refusing. We felt under a complete sense of siege in the Garvaghy Road and in effect we were. But what was the alternative? To allow the Orangemen to march all over the community, that would have had a very negative impact on the whole community. The RUC were brutal towards us, they beat us off the road and fired plastic bullets at people."

As time went on the protest also became a Mecca for loyalist paramilitaries from all over Northern Ireland. Each year there were shows of strength and in July 2000 Johnny Adair, the notorious UDA leader from Belfast went to Portadown and posed for cameras in front of armed and masked LVF men at a housing estate in the town.

While publicly Unionists refused to talk to the residents it had become clear that loyalist paramilitaries were directing the violence at Drumcree. David Trimble, leader of the Ulster Unionist Party, held secret talks with Billy Wright who was still advocating violence against Catholics. The talks angered nationalist residents whom he refused to meet, despite being the area's MP. In fact he didn't meet with the residents until 1999 when a delegation from the US Congress urged him to do so.

An Orangeman himself, he had very publicly sided with the marches when, in 1995, alongside Ian Paisley, he led the Orange Order march through the Garvaghy Road. Critics accused him of using his role in the march to cultivate a hard-line image to win support for his UUP leadership the next year.

Many observers believe the Orange Order has had its reputation damaged by its association with the violence around Drumcree. The organisation has split not only on sectarian lines but on political ones, since then. When in 2001 the local District Master, Harold Gracey, refused to condemn the violence it was read by many as a sign that the order, at least in Portadown, was tacitly supporting civil disorder.

As the head of the Orange Order in Portadown Harold Gracey has been one of the most controversial figures in the Drumcree dispute. He vowed to live in a caravan on the hill overlooking the Garvaghy Road until the Orange Order was allowed to march, but he abandoned the protest shortly after, due to serious health concerns.

Alongside Gracey the main spokesman for the Orange Order in Portadown was Davy Jones. A bearded civil servant he defends the rights of anyone to come and support the Orange Order. However he admits that the association with violence has marred the reputation of the Order and has deterred some Protestants from attending the protest.

"I don't think we could tell people to go away from the protest. That isn't what it is about. Protestants from all over the province supported the stand we were taking for our own civil and religious liberties. We can't call on people to support us and then start turning them away. Whatever someone's past or what they get up to away from Drumcree, all we asked was that they behaved themselves while they were there. We couldn't ask for any more than that. People were furious when the Order was banned from marching. Portadown is the birthplace of the Orange Order yet here we are in a situation where a group of Sinn Féin-backed people are telling us that we can't march down the road. It was right that we wouldn't talk to them because of that."

However, although the Orange Order has always insisted that the Garvaghy Road residents are unrepresentative of the area a survey carried out in 1996 in the Garvaghy Road area by the Independent Review of Parades, a British Government agency, found that 93% of the local population were sympathetic to the views expressed by the Residents' Coalition.

For Davy Jones and Orangemen like him the ban on Orange Parades on the Garvaghy Road is a sign that nationalists are gaining the upper hand in Northern Ireland. But he says that part of the blame for failing to reach a compromise with residents was a decree by the Grand Lodge of the Orange Order banning any dialogue with the Parades Commission. He argues that many in the Portadown Lodge would have been happy to talk to the Parades Commission and says deals have been sacrificed as part of a wider political game being played out in Northern Ireland.

"People blame the Portadown brethren for not reaching a compromise but that isn't fair at all. Personally I believe it would have been better to have talked to the Parades Commission, although there would have been no guarantee anything would have come out of it. But we were stopped from talking to the Parades Commission by the Orange Order Grand Lodge and that has to be remembered."

However, as the protest has dragged on there has been a closer flirtation between militant loyalists and senior figures in the Portadown Orange Order. The Drumcree stand off remained a rallying point for anti-Agreement Unionists as the pace of the peace process quickened in the late 1990's. Direct Unionist political support for the protest is now confined to the DUP and anti-agreement Unionists.

The annual standoffs also brought into question the role of the Church of Ireland in Northern Ireland. The Orange Order's association with the Church of Ireland stretches back to the Order's formation in 1790. Initially formed as a reaction against the efforts of the United Irishmen, a mainly Protestant group whose aim was to unite Irish people of all religions against English rule in Ireland, the Orange Order allowed only members of the Church of Ireland to join. The centuries old link was severely tested at Drumcree.

The use of the church ground by loyalists and Orangemen and the scenes of violence associated with it prompted the General Synod of the Church of Ireland to issue a decree in 1999 which would have effectively banned Orangemen from using the church during the dispute if it were implemented. Every July the graveyard and land surrounding Drumcree church was filled with Orangemen who would engage in running battles with the British Army and police.

The Synod called on all Orange Order members entering the church to obey an agreement which called for them to be orderly and not to engage in acts of civil disobedience. However the call was ignored in Portadown. The Rector of Drumcree Church, Rev. John Pickering, was accused of allowing the Orangemen to abuse Church property. Despite the criticism Rev. Pickering says he had no choice - to close the church doors would have been to deny a basic religious right.

"It is a very hard time of the year for everyone. What is happening here is a symptom of what is happening in Northern Ireland as a whole. The problem is that the Orangemen and indeed the residents felt that the problem at Drumcree was more than just a parade. Orangemen felt their parade and culture were being hit, that's what makes Drumcree big time. It is always a matter of anxiety when there are untoward things happening after the church sermon but when they leave the church they are on a public road. I make a distinction between the church and the trouble that breaks out afterward."

The Rev. Pickering has been accused by members of his own church and the Garvaghy Road residents of washing his hands of the problem by adopting this attitude. However he did hold talks with loyalists during the protests.

"Although the Synod did ask the Orangemen to sign up their response was that they were doing their best and they weren't breaking any laws."

Although the problem remains an open sore the protest at Drumcree appears to have petered out. It still attracts thousands of loyalists, but in recent years it has ended with only sporadic violence in parts of Belfast. Indeed by 2003 the protest was totally peaceful with only a few hundred turning up, presenting a letter of protest to the police on guard at temporary steel gates and then dispersing. In the weeks leading up to the 2003 march there was repeated talk of some sort of deal being done. However the Garvaghy Road residents denied being involved. What is clear, however, is that some Orangemen are openly saying that talks with residents are not out of the question, a situation similar to that in Derry City.

Undeniably tensions are raised during the annual Drumcree standoff, and the world's media descend on the Garvaghy road in hope of a story. But the once menacing threats from Loyalist leaders to bring Northern Ireland to its knees no longer have the same impact.

David Trimble, who many accuse of making his political career through Drumcree, doesn't attend the protest any longer - he wouldn't be welcome in any case. An example of how Trimble's standing has fallen among hard-line Unionists was on Westminster election night in 2001 when he had to be escorted away from a Portadown polling station when loyalists attacked him. Those politicians who lend credence to the protesters by attending are now explicitly anti-agreement Unionists.

Many argue that the heat has been taken out of the Drumcree dispute by advancements in the political process and by shifting attitudes amongst Protestants to the stand taken by the Orange Order. Breandán Mac Cionnaith says that after the Good Friday Agreement of 1998 Unionist politicians couldn't afford the same level of support to Drumcree because of political splits.

"In 1995, 1996 and 1997 the Unionist community was united against the peace process so the UUP and DUP could both support it, but the Good Friday Agreement changed that. After that Unionism was split between those who supported it and those who didn't so the whole political situation changed the level of support for Drumcree. It also became the unacceptable face of Unionism. Every year there was widespread violence because of it and some people in the Unionist community seemed to want to move away from it. Four years into a peace process Drumcree was the single event in the north that sparked off mass riots and trouble and the Orangemen at Drumcree were reliant on that to get their way. That isn't the case anymore."

Many have speculated that Drumcree was a body blow from which the Orange Order found it hard to recover. Political fault lines within Unionism were certainly opened up by the Good Friday Agreement.

Over the years several attempts have been made to reach agreement. In the summer of 1999, Portadown District Orange Order and other Unionists entered negotiations with the Garvaghy Road residents. Many considered the Unionists decision to talk without preconditions, a breakthrough. A draft proposal was agreed. It is claimed by a source close to events that this document went a long way to meeting the concerns of the Garvaghy residents. However, at a further meeting in Craigavon Civic Centre, held to clear up the formalities and minor details, the deal collapsed, despite the optimistic atmosphere immediately preceding the meeting.

Breandán Mac Cionnaith, according to Unionist sources, challenged the credentials of David Trimble to negotiate. He then raised the issue of Trimble's commitment to the Good Friday Agreement, which Unionist saw as irrelevant. There then ensued, apparently, a dispute as to what had actually been agreed in the draft document. The Garvaghy residents then left the meeting.

In 2000, Brian Currin, a respected South African lawyer with an impressive reputation for successful mediation in conflict situations, was persuaded to help resolve Drumcree. After months of cross negotiations, he had achieved significant co-operation and rapport with both the local Orange Order and the Garvaghy residents.

Early in 2001, Currin was confident enough to produce an in depth analysis, containing proposals he was encouraged to believe would impress both sides. However, much to his surprise, his report was rejected outright by the Orangemen's ruling body, The Grand Lodge Of Ireland. This particular episode has not been discussed in depth by the media. One disillusioned Unionist observer, who participated in some of these negotiations, adds an interesting postscript;

"Skilled negotiations in any dispute always aim for a 'win-win' solution, one that is acceptable to all. But there were some one the Loyalist side who wanted a 'winner takes all' result. These people insisted that a 'senior Unionists political figure', had to be given the credit for the successful resolution proposed by Currin, or they would block any deal. The public recognition would have boosted the standing of the 'Pro-Agreement' Unionists wing of the Ulster Unionist Party in its struggle with the 'Anti-Agreement' wing."

No tears were shed at Unionist Party Headquarters, when Brian Currin left Northern Ireland in frustration. A subsequent initiative to resurrect serious talks, using an international Conflict Resolution body, which would have included former US President Carter's Emissary, was abandoned. A new mediator, it was felt, would probably make a similar analysis and make similar recommendations to Currin's proposals – with a similar result.

• • • • • • • •

As things stand at the time of writing, Drumcree is not the issue it was a few years ago, as far as most of the North's population is concerned. However, as with all flashpoints in Northern Ireland, Drumcree still has the potential to become a focal point for disorder.

Chapter 8

Rural Hotspots – Dunloy and Bellaghy

The experience of marching disputes has played itself out in other rural areas of Northern Ireland over the past number of years. In rural areas where demographics were sometimes the result of forced plantation dating back to the 1600's the issue of Orange marches have proved just as controversial as in the inner-city areas of Belfast and Derry.

Two towns which came to the fore of the marching dispute in the mid-90's were Bellaghy and Dunloy, in counties Derry and Antrim respectively. Bellaghy is a small overwhelmingly nationalist town with a strong republican tradition. Its graveyard holds two of the most revered martyrs of the republican cause, cousins Tom McElwee and Francis Hughes who died on hunger strike in 1981. The town itself is more than 90% nationalist with a strong tradition of resistance of what it sees as to British rule dating back to the War of Independence in 1921. Seventy-five years later

Bellaghy residents were opposing the Loyal Order marches through their town.

Clashes between nationalists and Orangemen in the town were nothing new. In 1972 an Orange march in Bellaghy sparked a huge riot which lasted for two days. Until 1994 there was an average of four Loyal Order marches in the town every year, after the ceasefire the number of parades doubled. Bellaghy residents had made official protests against the parades in some form or another since 1983, but in 1996 matters came to a head when a tense standoff developed between residents and the Loyal Orders.

Egged on by the dispute at Drumcree the standoff ended in a riot in the town and running battles between the RUC and nationalists. The Orangemen's traditional route had seen them leave the Orange Hall, march through the Main Street and back again before arriving at the local Presbyterian Church. They were insistent that the route be kept and dismissed the residents' opposition as a Sinn Féin-orchestrated ploy to eradicate Orange culture from the town.

Initially they refused to talk to the residents, saying to do so would be to legitimise Sinn Féin. Bolstered by their success in 1995 when despite strong local opposition they were allowed to march the length of the town the Loyal Orders gathered members around the town.

The area's MP at the time was the DUP's Rev Willie McCrea. A staunch Unionist he became a hate-figure for nationalists in the area with many angered by his hard-line comments. When he shared a platform in Portadown with UVF killer Billy 'King Rat' Wright he further alienated himself from nationalists. His flirtation with loyalist paramilitaries stretched back to the mid 1980's and the Ulster Resistance. When Sinn Féin's Martin McGuinness took his parliamentary seat from him in the 1997 Westminster elections McCrea promised that Mid-Ulster would "reap a grim harvest".

Although they weren't allowed to march in 1996 a compromise was set up whereby the Royal Black Preceptory agreed to meet with the residents to discuss future parades. The meeting went ahead but it was the last one to ever take place. Jim Hassen is the spokesman for the Bellaghy residents group and met with the Royal Black Preceptory. He says it was a ridiculous situation since many of the Royal Black's members were also in the Orange Order and Apprentice Boys.

"The way we looked at it was this, we wanted to talk to all of them but the Royal Blacks agreed to meet us only once and that was all the meetings that ever took place. I don't see why they agreed to meet us wearing one hat but not another. The meeting came to very little anyway and since then they have refused to meet with us. We were very open to dialogue and still feel it is the best way to solve the problem and to have good community relations but that isn't shared by the Orangemen. This town was sick of being hemmed in from five o'clock at night until midnight every time the Orangemen wanted to march. It was ridiculous, Bellaghy is a 95% Catholic town yet we were put under curfew for whole evenings while people who wouldn't even talk to us paraded the town. They tried to make it out as though our opposition to Orange Parades was something that was only new, but that is nonsense. I have been involved in protests against Orange Order marches in Bellaghy stretching right back to 1983. We are glad that they no longer come into the town but if they want to talk to us they know where the door is."

The idea that nationalists only objected to parades in a post-ceasefire Northern Ireland is a commonly held view within Unionism. Unionists claim that the residents' campaigns are orchestrated by Sinn Féin and cite this as one reason they won't talk to them. Many Orangeman claim that before 1969 Catholics came to Orange Order marches, Catholics say that is wishful thinking. Willie McCrea was the DUP MP for the constituency in which Bellaghy was when the trouble broke out in 1996. As a prominent Orangeman and hardline Unionist he backed the Orange Order. He says that many of the Bellaghy residents hadn't the right to protests because a lot of them have "never worked a day in their life".

"Quite a lot of those people never even did a days work in their life; they never paid taxes and there they were out on the streets insulting ordinary people who had worked. We were disgusted by their protests. All our people wanted was the right to exercise their civil and religious liberties, nothing more than that. That's why we wouldn't talk to the residents. Why should we go crawling to them when it was clear they just wanted to take away our liberties. They were being told how to feel by Sinn Féin/IRA, and as for them being insulted that is a joke. They were coming from as far away as Belfast to be insulted, coming in by the bus load and the unionist people in this part of the world aren't stupid, and we knew what was going on. We held onto our principles and demanded the right to walk the Queen's Highway when other people were selling out. The parades commission was just another sop to republicanism; we have no faith in it whatsoever."

Although Willie McCrea's views appear vitriolic he says they sum up how most Orangemen in Bellaghy felt. He argues that to Orangemen the residents' protests were just the latest stage in an IRA campaign to drive Protestants out of the town.

"Protestants have been shot and killed in that town over the whole of the Troubles but we have still maintained a presence in it. Young lads were taken from their homes by the IRA and killed from the 1970's onwards just because they were Protestants. What the people behind the protests were trying to do was make sure that Bellaghy was a 100% Catholic town and we weren't for having that."

Sinn Féin's Martin McGuinness is the MP for the area

now and he emphasises how important talking is in resolving the issue.

"In Derry there was a will to make a deal, the residents were very keen that should be the case. The Royal Black and Orange Order didn't take that same sort of stance in Bellaghy. Over the past years things have been relatively peaceful there, but the difference with say there and Derry is that everyone wanted to engage in a meaningful way."

He does however recognise that sectarianism takes on a different form in the country. In rural areas people live through each other much more.

Unlike Bellaghy, Dunloy is an isolated Catholic town in North Antrim, with a population of just over 1,600 people. It lies just outside the Bible belt of Ballymena and all the major towns close to it such as Coleraine and Ballymoney are strongly Unionist. Its MP is Ian Paisley, himself an ardent advocate of the Loyal Orders' right to march and a supporter of the Orders' refusal to talk to residents.

It was in Ballymoney that the three Quinn children were burned to death on the Twelfth of July 1998 when loyalist petrol bombers targeted their home. Their deaths were linked to the parades disputes across the North, and nationalists in Dunloy, less than ten miles from the murders felt most vulnerable.

The protests against Orange marches in Dunloy began in 1995 when a team of GAA supporters from the village were attacked by an Orange parade when they returned from a match in Belfast. The incident sparked a riot in the town and as a result a residents committee was set up to oppose further marches.

Unlike other marching disputes in Northern Ireland Dunloy presented a special problem. Because of the town's geography the Orange March had either to be allowed to proceed in full or banned completely if the residents and Orangemen couldn't find a compromise. The last time an Orange March was forced through the town was in 1996, three years later a compromise between residents and the Loyal Orders meant a parade was allowed into the town on the understanding talks would take place afterwards. However the talks never took place and since then the Parades Commission has banned successive parades from the town.

Phillip McGuigan, a Sinn Féin councillor for Dunloy, says the worst year came in 1996 when the Drumcree dispute was at its height. For 24 hours loyalists surrounded the town, held back by a heavy RUC presence.

"Around 25 bus loads of loyalists came up the A26 and parked right opposite the village. They got out and surrounded the entire area. People in Dunloy were terrified, we felt very vulnerable. But the resident's opposition to the parades has always been based on the fact that the Loyal Orders refuse to talk to us. In 1999 we thought we had reached some form of compromise by allowing them to march down with the understanding that they would talk to us later. But they backed out of their promises and since then there has been no parades. As far as the residents are concerned talks are the only long-term solution to the parading dispute but at the same time they are happy the town is no longer the scene of Orange Marches which meant they were crewed into their homes for hours."

When the Orangemen were prevented from parading through Dunloy later in 1996 they staged a picket outside a Catholic Church in Bushmills in September 1996.

The idea of picketing rural Catholic churches as a bargaining tool for further parades caught on and in 1997 loyalists staged a 14 month long picket outside Harryville Catholic Church in Ballymena, pledging to maintain it until their brethren were allowed to march through Dunloy.

Mass-goers had eggs thrown at them and paint was daubed over the chapel and RUC men were called in to escort them through the crowds.

One of the key figures in the Harryville Protest was William McGaughey, a former life prisoner for the UVF. He was jailed in the 1970's for the murder of a Catholic chemist in the town. He had lured the victim from his bed by telling him he needed medicine for a sick child.

The Harryville protest was supported by the Dunloy Orange Accordion Band which turned up to play an impromptu concert for the crowd. Phillip McGuigan says that episode hardened attitudes in the Dunloy. "Some people felt that was the final nail in the coffin for Orange marches in the town. On the one hand the Orangemen were demanding the right to march through our town without even talking to us and then they sent their accordion band down to Ballymena to support people picketing Catholics going to mass."

Loyalists however insisted on linking mass-goers with Orange marches. They argued that if they were prevented from walking the 'Queen's Highway' to get to their places of worship, then Catholics going to mass would suffer the same fate. Davy Tweed is the Worshipful Grand Master of the Dunloy Orange Lodge and a DUP councillor in Ballymena. As a former Irish Rugby International turned politician he is a well-known figure in North Antrim. He took part in the protests at Dunloy and Harryville. He says loyalists felt protesting at Harryville was something they had a right to do.

"I only actually took part in the protests at Harryville a few times, but like most Unionists I regarded it as legitimate. The situation there and the one at Dunloy were the same. At the end of the day Orangemen in Dunloy were prevented from going to their place of worship and we were making the point that Catholics were allowed to walk to mass in mainly loyalists towns.

"People in Ballymena were showing their support for the Brethren in Dunloy that is all. We were gutted when the Dunloy people objected to us marching, we couldn't understand why. We thought we had a good relationship with the people in Dunloy but their residents group was adamant that we weren't going to march. Now a lot of Protestants would see Dunloy as a republican village, which is no-go for Protestants."

Since the first protest was held neither side have held talks with the other. The Dunloy residents say they are open to talks but the Loyal Orders have refused to negotiate. Davy Tweed says they feel under no obligation to seek the consent of local residents when applying to march.

"We had and still have a viewpoint that it isn't necessary to discuss our marches with the residents. From our point of view the whole campaign was orchestrated by republicans and so as far as we can see there is no point in talking to them."

The policy of no talks has led to the Parades Commission imposing a ban on the Loyal Orders marching in Dunloy. Some Loyal Orders such as the Apprentice Boys have met with residents groups on a regular basis, with Derry being the best example. As mentioned before an agreement between residents and the Apprentice Boys has meant a compromise which allows the Apprentice Boys to parade on the city walls and through the city centre. There is a tacit understanding among the Loyal Orders that refusing to talk to residents in places such as Dunloy almost invariably means no walks. As the Worshipful Grand Master of Dunloy Orange Lodge Davy Tweeds accepts this but says Orangemen must stick to their principles.

"We don't know what the future holds for us but no matter what happens we have to try to survive. We have always been peaceful and hopeful that people in Dunloy will see sense. We understand that there are two traditions in Dunloy but just as we respect the Catholic one, they must respect ours too."

The DUP MP for Londonderry, Gregory Campbell, is a member of both the Orange Order and Apprentice Boys. He supports the Apprentice Boys decision to talk to the Bogside Residents but say he understands why the Loyal Orders refused to have dialogue in Dunloy. He says that sectarian tensions increased in the period when opposition to marches in Dunloy was at its strongest.

"I think it would be fair to say that the area suffered from a higher degree of sectarianism throughout that time. It definitely brought the whole issue to the fore. But people in and around these towns have worked hard to make sure that it has died away. I think nationalists need to respect Protestant rights."

Although no face to face talks took place there were some backdoor negotiations under the auspices of the mediation network but little came out of it. Around a dozen times a year the Loyal Orders attempt to march from the Orange Hall in Dunloy to the church. They are routinely blocked by the police and duly hand over a letter of protest stating that their civil and religious liberties are being denied by the Parades Commission. Dunloy residents no longer come out to protest.

In the years when Dunloy and Bellaghy were in the news other rural areas such as Keady in County Armagh, Newtownbutler in County Fermanagh and Strabane in County Tyrone, amongst around a dozen other areas, held protests against marches by the Loyal Orders.

While all the cases mentioned in this book involved the Loyal Orders marching in areas where there was nationalist opposition there is one case where local Unionists have opposed a nationalist march by the Ancient Order of Hibernians, a nationalist Catholic organisation which traditionally marches on St. Patrick's Day (17 March) and on the Feast of the Assumption (15 August). This happened in the town of Kilkeel, a town with a Protestant majority but with a substantial Catholic minority. The arguments were more or less similar with the nationalist saying they had a right to march to the town centre while the loyalist said that the area through which they wanted to march was Protestant. Some of the protesters did however say that their permission did not have to be sought and that the protests would cease as soon as the nationalist protests against loyalist marches ended.

• • • • • • • •

In such situations, where this reversal of roles occurs, people, whether marchers or protesters, are often confronted with the fact that they are espousing views often espoused by "the other side". One wonders for example if the AOH in Kilkeel received advice from the Garvaghy Road Residents' Coalition along the lines of "...seek consent for your march through dialogue...". And, perhaps the Portadown lodge of the Orange Order sent messages of support to the Kilkeel AOH, encouraging them to "do all that is necessary to walk the Queen's highway". Then again, perhaps not.

However, these comments show that some people at least can adopt as their own a view diametrically *opposed* to their own under certain conditions. Some contributors to this book admit that such contradictions force them to think a little differently on occasions.

Chapter 9
The Future

"Its co-existence or no existence"
Bertrand Russell

Many people, living outside interface areas, often form the impression that such conflict between alleged Christian communities is simply irrational violence, inspired by bigotry and hatred. Whatever the motivation for the often extreme violence, real or supposed, the vulnerable and innocent are often the victims of beatings, bombings and killings.

Such a harrowing, depressing scenario inevitably invites the reaction, "A plague on both your houses", a sentiment expressed by Reginald Maudling, when, as an early Ulster Secretary of State on a flight back to London after his initial visit to Northern Ireland, exclaimed: "What a bloody awful country. Fetch me a whiskey for God's sake."

Justified? Well, there are other, more positive,

perspectives. Visitors to Northern Ireland pay generous, unsolicited tribute to its citizens as the most hospi-
table, open and friendly as could be met anywhere in
the world. An impression is also gained of a better
quality of life and more relaxed social environment;
less serious crime; a superior education system; cour-
teous services and a unique level of community involvement in voluntary activities - not to mention the
beautiful scenery, on every doorstep and from every
window, leaving a magnificent vista in the minds of all
who leave these shores. So the notion that this part of
Ireland is somehow irrevocably conditioned to violence
and hatred is contradicted on many levels.

Can such a paradox be reconciled with the media
image? Despite these apparent contradictions, are
there seeds of hope that two 'warring' communities
can aspire to a harmonious, peaceful future, where
the present burning issues, which foment strife, would
be irrelevant and just a bad memory. Thankfully there
is a growing body of evidence to indicate that the
unthinkable is possible and that the province is edg-
ing inexorably, albeit slowly, toward a more stable
political era. And with a date for elections for the
Stormont Assembly now set, local people will at least
have the facilities and opportunity to govern themselves and taking responsibility for problem solving at
executive level. After all, if those at the top of the legislative chain cannot talk to each other sensibly, what
lead can they legitimately offer those in society in

general and interface areas in particular. Of course, having the elections take place in itself is no guarantee that an Executive will be set up. But it does mean such an Executive is one step closer to existing.

Away from the headline grabbing media reports of the relatively few flashpoint confrontations, an undisputed fact is that everyday life in Northern Ireland passes more normally than it did prior to the ceasefires of nearly a decade ago. The number of interface disputes, without underplaying their impact on communities, should be judged in the context of the wider Catholic and Protestant population relationships. At many levels of social interaction - the workplaces, the arts, leisure or business, sectarian bigotry or friction is notably absent. The sharing of non-contentious activities and, crucially, freedom from actual or implicit threat, is perhaps part of the explanation.

The significance, and the extent, of such peaceful association between so-called divided communities could be, in the view of many, more widely acknowledged and reported.

• • • • • • • •

Interviews for this book revealed that even in the midst of violent turmoil, dedicated organizations or individuals with no political agenda are working, often against great odds, to defuse dangerous situations or build closer cross-community understanding. We've seen, in 2003, a relatively peaceful summer in most interface areas - a result perhaps of the many behind the scenes activity of local people alluded to in this book. Inter-church and secular groups are striving to bridge the barriers of mistrust that divide an essentially similar people. Individually or collectively, spontaneous gestures of goodwill are demonstrated. One such example was a donation of £10,000 raised by five Catholic parishes in North Belfast towards rebuilding Whitehouse Presbyterian Church destroyed in a sectarian arson attack. Likewise when loyalists damage Catholic churches, the local Protestant communities have not been found wanting in expressing sympathy and offering financial assistance. Such instances, while seemingly not as dramatic in a news context, are real, everyday events in even hard-line interface areas.

However, improving 'inter-tribal' relationships at flashpoint areas, commendable and vital though it may be, cannot alone resolve entrenched political divisions, or the conflict of identity and national allegiances. Few will disagree with one spokesman's analysis: "The violence surrounding Glenbryn and the Holy Cross dispute are a microcosm of the whole conflict in the North". There are many who would say that the biggest interface factor of them all is the whole concept of Partition, with its attendant pros and cons.

The initiative for radical change must therefore come from the major unionist-loyalist/nationalist-republican groupings. They have to acknowledge the changing demographic, economic and political landscape. If left to politicians alone and, if the old parameters which prevailed and shaped the course of Ulster politics pre-1969 still existed, the province's future would be a bleak one indeed. However after decades of near-civil war and thousands of deaths, the parameters have moved. Forces and trends over which local politicians have no influence are now at work. These will determine the future.

Reassessments

At the core of the North's conflict are fundamental factors that have been significantly changed in recent years. Inter-party negotiations for a restored Assembly and its institutions have seen a date for elections agreed by both the Irish and British governments. If the core issues are dealt with by the politicians, with realism tempered by a degree of trust and generosity, then a workable new Agreement could emerge. Some will challenge the premises posed below, but who can dispute the old cliché, "Politics is the art of the possible".

• • • • • • • •

Many in the Protestant population acknowledge that Northern Ireland is now regarded as the problem offspring, rather than a legitimate member, of the British family of nations. Cabinet minister's routinely reiterate the former Northern Ireland Secretary, Peter Brook's early 1990's statement that, "Britain had no strategic or economic interest in the province". This is hardly reassuring to a country, whose majority population always identifies itself culturally and politically with the United Kingdom. Such perceptions, allied to poor leadership, fragmented Unionism and perceived republican political gains have generated a loss of confidence and uncertainty for the unionists' future in the 'six counties'.

Conversely, similar doubts are shared by many Catholics. They detect the Republic's enthusiasm for a 32-County Ireland has diminished considerably and for a number of reasons. Many years of northern paramilitary warfare and associated mafia-style activities have reaped a grim economic and human toll. Why, some ask, import it to the Republic along with one million recalcitrant Protestants and thousands of Catholics disenchanted with remote Dublin rule?

Profound economic factors also mitigate against the case for unity, as far as most Protestant and pro-union Catholics are concerned. There is the precedent of German reunification. West Germany, the wealthiest of European states, is today facing serious economic problems after absorbing the former Communist East Germany. Ireland, a smaller nation, would, many feel, fare no better. As a member of the European Union (E.U.) the Republic received financial benefits, which assisted the birth of the Celtic Tiger. However, the Celtic Tiger appears to many to have lost some momentum. Irish unity, even with the consent of the unionists, would, according to some economists, produce massive constitutional and economic upheaval that The Republic of Ireland is perhaps ill prepared to sustain. While the Dail pays 'lip service' to the concept of Irish unity, many feel it will not pursue that goal with the old vigour. Even many senior politicians in the Republic of Ireland suggest that pragmatism (rather than idealism) favours 'the North' remaining British, enjoying trading, cultural and some political links with 'the South.

In the context of the E.U., the case for 'nationalisms' could be perceived to have been weakened. Nation state authority is increasingly vested in Brussels. As a result, the Irish model, which envisaged 'Four Green Fields' of economic and cultural independence divorced from foreign domination, is arguably unachievable.

Of course, it's not just the traditional nationalist premise that has to be challenged. Unionists must make difficult reassessments too. Catholics with a significant electoral mandate must be encouraged to play a pivotal and equal role in all strata of government. It must be admitted that the old mantra "No power sharing with Catholics" is today seldom publicly voiced. There should be a wider recognition that not all Catholics are overt or covert 'subversives'. And even if republicans (or anyone else for that matter) continue to describe themselves as 'revolutionaries', as long as they have a democratic mandate, they should be free to purse their stated aims and be included in all bodies to which they are elected - assuming they have declared themselves committed to peaceful and democratic means. Recent statements from Sinn Féin's Gerry Adams, after talks with the Unionist leader, David Trimble, suggest to many that Irish Republicanism concurs with this view.

Misconceptions of each side are a major obstacle to political progress. A more honest and generous acknowledgement from unionists of the contributions the SDLP and Sinn Féin have made to the present improved political climate, despite nationalism's own internal difficulties, would not be misplaced. The decision to recognise and enter devolved government at Stormont - the despised bastion of unionist / British rule in Ireland - was itself a radical shift from the traditional nationalist position. The implicit declaration that the 'armed struggle' cannot achieve Irish unity, that persuasion and negotiation with guarantees for Protestants was the way forward, also indicates a new realism and maturity among nationalists and republicans. Have unionists grasped this?

Protestants have to address the status and levels of courtesy they accord to Irish culture and traditions within Northern Ireland. These have a dynamism and richness as equally valid as the Ulster / British ones. Irish street names, a 'foreign incomprehensible language' may rankle with 'the loyalist psyche', but these are treasured symbols of a proud people. If the North genuinely aspires to be a modern, pluralist society at peace with itself, then the diversity of culture in the two main communities must be equally promoted. Quebec, Canada, a city with similar problems of dual allegiances resolved the issue many years ago. National government rests in Ottawa but the French tradition in the city and Quebec Province is very evident. In fact, one could say that our differences should not just be timidly 'tolerated' but positively 'celebrated'.

Hard-line nationalists will find some facts as disconcerting as their loyalist opponents. Some demographic authorities project that, due to its birth rate falling to a par with Protestants, the Catholic population becoming the majority is no longer the 'inevitability' it was once considered to be. At most, according to such analysis, parity in the religious head count might occur. If true, this demolishes the long-standing Protestant phobia of nationalists 'breeding and voting' them out of the Union. Such projections are reinforced by the contention that a significant section of the Catholic community will oppose change to the status quo. The 1998 Good Friday Agreement also removed part of the *raison d'être* for Irish unity. As a condition of the Agreement the Republic's constitutional claim over Northern Ireland was renounced in a public referendum. And if the Republic of Ireland government can have a new found tolerance of the status quo, then, so goes the argument, at least some northern nationalists will too.

Do grounds for optimism exist to the degree that one day the North will have a fully integrated, diverse community enjoying peaceful co-existence? And will the Drumcree, Holy Cross, and similar issues, with their associated pipe bombs and intimidations, simply fade into the past? The Good Friday Agreement, deliberately fudged by all parties and two governments in order to reach a consensus, was a brave experiment to break the political deadlock. It attempted to accommodate diverse and seemingly irreconcilable political and national aspirations. With hindsight, it was always going to be a fragile consensus that needed time to evolve in order to confounded its critics. The decommissioning issue was its perhaps fatal flaw. For many unionists, the failure of the IRA to 'honour commitments' to disarm sabotaged the vital element of the Agreement - trust. Republicans for their part complained that they were being asked to disarm while loyalists had not only stated that they had no intention of decommissioning but were not even on ceasefire. Nor had the British 'securicrats' lessened their activity, from a republican perspective. Decommissioning, they argued, was a two way street.

From community workers in interface areas, to Stormont ministers, trust is the most sought after commodity. Trust is the prerequisite for all new agreements, whether on the streets or in the corridors of power.

In future talks for restoring devolved local government, lessons of the 'failed' Assembly will be crucial. Behind the public rhetoric and invective against their opponents, serious reappraisal of objectives and strategies must already be taking place among the major parties. Strong leadership is required to confront and embrace the many unpalatable realities of the day. One hope might be that the brief experience of government in the Assembly with decision-making and financial responsibility is incentive enough to modify the more extreme political ambitions on both sides.

We often hear the comment, "Northern Ireland's problems are impossible to solve". But the impossible can happen. The once invincible Soviet Union collapsed almost overnight when its Superpower strategy could not be sustained in the modern world and when its citizens demanded change. Today the Cold War is over. Former enemies, the USA and Russia, have a close international and economical relationship. Are Northern Ireland's difficulties really more intractable?

The introduction to this book records 'surprise and horror' at what Irishmen are inflicting on fellow Irishmen. Others, with some confidence, anticipate a different and better future for their country. It could be a country still with a close link to Britain but which will have a new mutually acceptable identity and whose constitution would enshrine the principles of mutual respect and tolerance. Cultures and traditions, which today divide, could be shared by old enemies and absorbed into the ethos of a New Northern Ireland. On the other hand, Northern Ireland could gradually become more comfortable with its 'Irishness' and choose to be a region of Ireland, one with a unique and distinctively British cultural heritage, protected by a new constitution that would recognise it's particular independence with some acceptable degree of autonomy.

Assuming the politicians (who generally don't live in interface areas) can show courageous leadership and can offer trust with as much passion as they demand it, then the restored Assembly can fulfil its intended function of letting the people decide; people who aspire to be Irish, British, Ulster; Catholic Protestant and Dissenter. It is the view of the editorial contributors to this book that the politicians owe all the people in the North, but especially those in interface areas, workable and robust political institutions. Otherwise, those at the front line of Ulster's divisions, those in interface areas, will continue be the most likely victims of political power vacuums.

This is the challenge facing Ulster politicians in the coming months. A war weary people yearning to live peacefully with their fellow countrymen demand it. With generosity and vision those politicians can deliver it.

Richard Bingham

Glossary

CIRA - Continuity IRA. Offshoot of the PIRA. Came to prominence in 1996 when it bombed the Killyhelvin hotel in Enniskillen. Remains opposed to the GFA but considered by many to be peripheral in republican circles. Considered politically close to Republican Sinn Féin, which split from the Provisional Republican movement in 1986.

CRUA - Concerned Residents of Upper Ardoyne.

DUP - Democratic Unionist Party. (Founded and led by Rev Ian Paisley. Considered to be more 'hard-line' than the Ulster Unionist Party).

GFA - Good Friday Agreement. (Signed in 1998 by both the Irish and British governments as well as three parties of the four main parties, Sinn Féin, SDLP, UUP. The DUP refused to sign up and still oppose the Agreement, as do many in the UUP).

GRC - Garvaghy Road Residents Coalition (Chairman Breandán Mac Cionnaith).

INLA - Irish National Liberation Army. Republican para-military grouping, originally formed in the early 1970s around members of the Official IRA and others. Never a 'mainstream' republican group although it achieved some 'spectaculars' during the Troubles, such as killing Airey Neave in the House Of Commons car park in 1979 and the killing of LVF leader Billy Wright in the Maze prison in 1997.

IRA - Irish Republican Army (throughout this book, the term IRA applies to the organisation also known as the Provisional IRA). By far the dominant force in Irish republican paramilitary circles. Also referred to as PIRA and, the Provos).

LOCC - Lower Ormeau Concerned Community. Residents committee founded in the mid 1990s to protest against loyalist marches. Gerard Rice would possibly be its most publicly recognised member, being spokesman.

LVF - Loyalist Paramilitary grouping, originally formed in 1996 around Portadown Loyalist Billy Wright, when it split from the UVF. The LVF opposed the UVF's continuance of its 1994 ceasefire.

MLA - Member of the Legislative Assembly. The Assembly was created by the Good Friday Agreement and devolved power to Northern Ireland from Westminster in the UK. MLAs are effectively MPs of the devolved Assembly.

NIO - Northern Ireland Office. Westminster government's political and civic presence in Northern Ireland.

PSNI - Police Service Of Northern Ireland (the successor to the RUC).

PUP - Progressive Unionist Party. Loyalist political party led by David Ervine. Also prominent in the PUP is Billy Hutchison. Both are elected MLAs. Political advisers to the UVF.

RIRA - Real IRA. Split from the Provos in Oct 1997. Opposed to GFA.

RUC - Royal Ulster Constabulary 1921–2000.

SDLP - Social Democratic and Labour Party (Lead for many years by John Hume, now by Mark Durkan. For many years the SDLP was the main catholic/nationalist party. Recently has been challenged for that position by Sinn Fein, which now has more Westminster MPs than the SDLP, 4 to 3.)

UDA - Ulster Defence Association. Main loyalist paramilitary grouping formed in the early 1970s to patrol loyalist areas in the perceived absence of law and order when the Troubles were at their height.

UFF - Ulster Freedom Fighters. 'Military wing' of the UDA

UUP - Ulster Unionist Party (Main unionist/protestant party. Recently challenged by DUP for that role).

UVF - Ulster Volunteer Force. Loyalist paramilitary grouping with fewer members than the UDA although some loyalists consider the UVF to be smaller through choice and more of an 'select' organisation than the UDA.